again, Anthony and Anna's story shows how nothing is impossible to God.

It is a story that begins with Anthony doing time for attempted murder, having long before come to the conclusion that life itself was meaningless and finding no good reason for living it thereafter with any obvious morals or scruple. In prison, that darkest of places, the light of Christ peered in unexpectedly and stood before Anthony to offer him a different way, a fresh hope and a new life. By God's grace Anthony made the hard choices that brought him back to the Christian faith of his birth but now in an entirely new way. He found himself born again into a faith he had previously known but now as the event of a living encounter with Jesus that made the same faith entirely new.

Anthony's story is the story of the glory of the Holy Spirit working through all His Christian communities. Anthony's salvation came through evangelical Protestant disciples of the Lord whom the Spirit continues to use to this day to bring Anthony and Anna life and mission. These good disciples have supported Anthony and Anna in making their journey back to the Catholic faith in the diocese of Paisley where I am bishop. I remain profoundly grateful to our evangelical brothers and sisters in the Lord whom I love with great esteem and affection as real brethren in Christ. I am convinced the story of Anthony's miraculous conversion is a testimony of the Holy Spirit's power and a prophecy that He means soon to make all the brethren of Christ one."

Bishop John Keenan, Bishop of Paisley

"This is the authentic story of Anthony Gielty's remarkable conversion from a life of violence and crime to becoming a follower of Jesus. It is told with brutal honesty and raw emotion. The poignant descriptions

of his ongoing struggles with shame rather than guilt add to its credibility. What is fascinating about this account of his new faith journey is how he has been so profoundly influenced by different Christian traditions. What we see is a man of passion who speaks as an evangelical, feels as a charismatic and acts as a Catholic."

The Very Rev. Dr Trevor W.J. Morrow (Former Moderator of the Presbyterian Church in Ireland)

"This is a riveting book, that we read over two evenings. The first half is an ever-deeper pit of despair, and the second an ever-growing triumph of hope. People often wonder 'Where is God?' We urge you to read Anthony's well-written answer to Jesus knocking on his door. Here is one person's path to the peace he would never have known without Jesus. Here is encouragement for us all. We recommend this book with all our hearts."

Barry and Margaret Mizen, campaigners, speakers and founders of the Jimmy Mizen Foundation

"A challenging story of how an ordinary teenager ended up as a dangerous criminal, and whose life was transformed through the practice of traditional Christian devotions and the example of a medieval saint."

John Drane, theologian and author

More used to helping people change by rearranging their faces with his fists, and several other deadly weapons, Anthony Gielty's story of his transformation powerfully shows the amazing influence of prison chaplains, visitors and individuals who believe that nobody is beyond God's ability to remake a life.

This is a hugely challenging but moving story of conversion, not least because his wonderfully complex spiritual journey sees him return to his Catholic roots, experience charismatic renewal, become passionately evangelical then go on to Bible college in order to serve in evangelism.

Tony was a brutal young thug – the stuff of your nightmares. Anthony, however, after God had worked a miracle in him, is a walking example of God's grace and power. And you can meet both of him in this well-crafted and extraordinary book.

Out of the Darkness *could be* The Cross and the Switchblade *for this generation in its influence.*

Rev. Alan Sorensen; multi-award winning broadcaster and Church of Scotland minister

"Towards the end of his amazing story, Anthony Gielty writes about his two young sons and says that they are 'a reminder of God's blessing and ability to accomplish the unbelievable.' It's a phrase that sums up this book which is nothing less than that – a reminder of God's blessing and ability to accomplish the unbelievable.

"It's a book that will challenge the atheist who says there is no God. But it's a book that will equally challenge the believer who would limit God to one church tradition or one narrow expression of doctrine. To borrow a couplet from an old hymn, this book gloriously witnesses to the truth that 'the love of God is greater than the measure of man's mind, and the heart of the eternal is most wonderfully kind.' The story of Anthony Gielty is a heart-warming, spirit-enriching, mind-expanding testimony to God's amazing, life-transforming grace.

"Read it and rejoice!"

Chick Yuill, international speaker and former Salvation Army officer

Out of the Darkness

The transformation of one of Scotland's
most violent prisoners

Anthony Gielty

MONARCH
BOOKS

Oxford, UK, and Grand Rapids, USA

Published by Monarch Books
an imprint of
Lion Hudson plc
Wilkinson House, Jordan Hill Road,
Oxford OX2 8DR, England
Email: monarch@lionhudson.com
www.lionhudson.com/monarch

ISBN 978 0 85721 771 4
e-ISBN 978 0 85721 772 1

First edition 2016

Acknowledgments
Unless otherwise indicated, Scripture quotations are from The
Holy Bible, English Standard Version® (ESV®) copyright © 2001
by Crossway, a publishing ministry of Good News Publishers. All
rights reserved.
Scripture quotations marked GNB are from the Good News Bible
© 1994 published by the Bible Societies/HarperCollins Publishers
Ltd UK, Good News Bible© American Bible Society 1966, 1971,
1976, 1992. Used with permission.

Names have been changed to protect both the innocent and the
guilty.

A catalogue record for this book is available from the British
Library

Printed and bound in Great Britain by
Marston Book Services Ltd, Oxfordshire

Tighearnan Gielty
8 October 2013–28 August 2014

*"... I shall go to him, but he will not
return to me."*

2 Samuel 12:23b

He lived among the tombs. And no one could bind him any more, not even with a chain, for he had often been bound with shackles and chains, but he wrenched the chains apart, and he broke the shackles in pieces. No one had the strength to subdue him. Night and day among the tombs and on the mountains he was always crying out and cutting himself with stones. And when he saw Jesus from afar, he ran and fell down before him.

Mark 5:3–6 (ESV UK)

Contents

Acknowledgments

I acknowledge the terrible damage, pain and injustice of my evil actions. The bitterest years of my life could never atone for the suffering I have caused. With all my heart, I abhor my crimes and detest the destructive life I lived. I am so sorry to everyone that the evil of my life has reached: family, friends and especially old enemies – Tony is dead.

So much gratitude is due to Ali Hull for sticking with this book from day one. There's no way it would have been completed without your gentle perseverance, and not so gentle prodding. Thank you for believing in its worth and making the book what it is now.

Many thanks are due to Dr Derek Newton. In the midst of astonishing adversity and brutal life challenges, he took the time to read through his student's manuscript, sharpening and shaping it with his brilliant insight and advice.

My friend Professor Stuart Reid took me in not long after I left prison, and this book was begun under his roof. I really appreciate you not kicking me out, even when I burned your kitchen, broke your car, constantly left the house unlocked and pretty much shaved ten years off your life. Who would have thought a guy leaving years in jail would have been such a blessing? You're welcome, mate. All for Jesus.

Finally, to my wife Anna, this has been such a journey for you. Through constant illness, you have been an unfailing support. When I had no strength, your indefatigable commitment to our Saviour always inspired and roused me to write, preventing this book's pages from perishing. Who else could face month after month of uncertain days in hospital with our boys and yet still come in and demand that the work of the manuscript go on? Your steadfastness, and commitment to truth, along with your gentleness and kindness, charted a course right through the darkest of memories, refusing to quit, until they were put under Christ. I love you.

Prologue

HMP Glenochil

The atmosphere was charged on the wing that night, as we opened up for recreation.

"Tony, give me a blade," said Matt.

"Come with me," I replied, beckoning him to follow me to my cell.

Matt knew I would have a tool for him. I'd promised him a long, sharpened screwdriver – more of a spike. Yet as he followed me to my stash, my thoughts still harassed me, reminding me of the other path in life I had recently been considering. This path demanded non-violence. I quickly dismissed these thoughts and called for Matt to come to the back of my cell. "It's in here."

I set about breaking open my stereo. In no time I had freed the awful-looking tool and gave it to him. Instantly, a sly smirk flashed across his face. I knew he was picturing the terrible injuries he would be able to inflict.

We knew the drill. Often in Scottish prisons it's expected that if one of your mates is fighting, it is your duty, as one belonging to the same camp, to back him up. Both our camp and theirs had agreed that the scrap would kick off at recreation. We were all ready for it. As soon as

13

the screws let us out of the cells, every prisoner was on full alert. Everything and everyone was studied closely: facial expressions, conversations, nuances in expression, tone, and especially body language – all were examined. As expected, one of the other camp members came toward me, a man called John MacDonagh. He approached cautiously and seemed anxious, but not hostile.

"Tony, this is mental. There's no point in all of us getting involved in this."

"You know we're up for it, John."

"So are we, but what's the point in all of us getting diggered up and sent to every corner of Scotland?"

His appeal was unusual but not entirely unheard of. Men serving long sentences are all too familiar with what happens when trouble kicks off. Everyone thought to have had the slightest involvement in stabbings or slashings is dragged off to solitary, then they are scattered across the country's jails. Even when the investigation has been completed, those exonerated can still be left for months in the digger.

"Speak to your troops and see what you all want to do," John said, turning to go back to his camp.

"Fine."

After walking back to Matt and my men I informed them of the details of the conversation. "They're keen to keep damage to a minimum. They want to know if it can stay a square go." I looked up at Matt, "It's your call, bro."

"I'm easy!" he replied, oozing confidence.

"Right then," I said, and gave the other camp the nod.

Brad indicated to Matt which cell they should go into to "settle it". Matt followed him until they reached the cell, situated halfway along the wing. From the outside nothing could be seen. There were no cameras and, behind the doors, nowhere to run. As they both went in, the steel cell door was slammed shut behind them. Prisoners on the wing continued their pool games and conversations as if nothing was happening.

Groans could be heard that were at first barely audible, then they grew louder and louder. Suddenly, the cell door flew open and another prisoner, a lifer called Dane, ran out. He was injured and clutching his hand in pain. As soon as I spied Dane running out of the cell, I knew Matt had been set up. Dane was part of Brad's camp. I ran into the cell and found Matt staggering, with Brad backing off.

When Matt had walked into the cell, he had been grabbed from behind by Dane, who had been waiting unseen. Wrapping one arm around Matt's neck in a chokehold, he had him trapped. Brad then started to stab Matt with his blade. Matt tried to defend himself but could do little while struggling to breathe, and thus was stabbed again and again. In his attempts to shield himself from the oncoming blade, he was stabbed through his hands, while another blow slashed the top of his head when Brad tried to stab his skull. In the midst of this set-up, Matt had somehow managed to manoeuvre his arm and wound Dane with his screwdriver. This had sent him running out the door.

I hastily dragged Matt into the cell next door to see what the damage was. The head injury was severe, causing him to bleed so badly and so fast that I immediately made a bandage for him by ripping the sheets of the bedding in the cell. I tied it around his forehead in an attempt to stem the flow of blood, which was pouring out.

"I've just been done a beauty," Matt said.

I tried to reassure him, and again turned my attention

15

to stemming the bleeding from his head. Already it had soaked through the makeshift bandage. Blood was now running down his forehead into his eyes and mouth.

"Man, I'm done," he kept repeating. "Look at me! I've been done a cracker!"

He ripped off his top. "LOOK AT ME, MAN. I'M DONE!" he yelled, as he revealed the horrors of his injuries.

Flaps of skin were opening and closing as his chest heaved short, sharp breaths. These puncture wounds were allowing blood to freely ooze out and cascade down his body. Some of the wounds resembled small incisions; others were like cuts and scratches. They all leaked blood which was flowing down his body and onto the floor.

"We need to get you out of here, mate," I said, still in shock at seeing him in such a state.

"Tony, make sure you get them for this."

"Look at me. Give me the tool," I said, taking the screwdriver off him. "We need to get this place cleaned up before you go." Matt had to get medical attention immediately, yet the old rules meant I would take the weapon off him and clean the cell first, thus ensuring there would be minimal evidence for the police. Only after that could he go to the hospital. Such was the darkness of our criminal mentality – we didn't even want our worst enemies to be caught by the police.

I had no doubt in my mind that if Matt didn't get to a hospital soon, he would die. I sprinted to the mop cupboard and grabbed a mop and bucket and some cleaning materials. Making my way back to the cell, I tried to be as discreet as possible. The atmosphere on the wing was still extremely tense. Every one of the cons knew what had happened, yet all were united in their determination not to let the screws know.

As I re-entered the cell, John was there, the man who had set the whole thing up. He had his back to me and was gloating over Matt. Fury began to master me, and John had no idea of the danger he was in now that I had returned.

"Who do you think you are, coming up from the YOs, trying to get smart?" John mocked.

Matt was by now considerably weaker, and each moment was taking its toll on him. But John wasn't going to stop his triumphant abuse. "Look at you now…"

His words were drowned out by the thoughts that flew at me: *Who does he think he is? He set this whole thing up and now he's adding insult to injury. There are no cameras in here. I've got him now. This is the perfect opportunity! I'll say he tried to kill Matt, then went for me. Self-defence!*

As John continued his insults, I quietly closed the steel door behind me. Rage coursed through my body with every pulse. Unrestricted hatred consumed me.

HIS NECK! STICK THE SCREWDRIVER THROUGH HIS NECK! my thoughts screamed at me.

The screwdriver was held by my waistband under my T-shirt. I slowly grabbed hold of it. *Now the tables have turned. You have nowhere to run, and nobody can see what I am going to do to you.*

As I gently took the screwdriver from within my waistband, the flood of hatred and rage grew stronger with every breath. I sharpened my focus on the point where I would plunge the tool. Then, right before I made the strike, I looked over at Matt to signal my intentions. I wanted him to witness this payback first-hand.

1

Meaningless, Meaningless

"HURRY UP AND GET HERE!" Dad shouted down the phone to the emergency services. My baby brother was turning blue. Mum kept screaming his name, "JAMES! JAMES!" By throwing cold water on his face she eventually managed to bring him back to consciousness, but he had gone too long without oxygen and would be left permanently brain-damaged.

I grew up as part of a loving family, with two older sisters, Noreen and Sinéad, along with my twin brother Michael and my little brother James. Dad was an agricultural contractor to farms and, thanks to his work, we lacked nothing. Mum was kept extremely busy looking after us, especially James, who needed a lot of care. However, he was the happiest out of us all. Although psychologically impaired, he was as physically strong and fit as the rest of us. Even today he still shines with so much joy and contentment.

For the first seven years of my life, our family lived in a small mining village called Rosewell in Midlothian, about ten miles outside Edinburgh. Almost all of our extended family lived here. It was awesome. We were surrounded by lots of cousins, aunts, and uncles. "Bored" wasn't a word we understood. We spent our time playing football or exploring the surrounding countryside, and we were always there for each other. There was such a strong sense of community. As kids, the village was the centre of the world. Everything and everyone was there.

Apart from James, we all went to the local primary school, St Matthews. My very first day at school was eventful. The teachers allowed Michael and me to play in the sandpit situated just outside the classroom, in the arts and crafts hall. Unfortunately, they left us alone. In their absence Michael and I, along with the other proud new primary pupil Gareth, decided to redecorate the entire room, ceilings and all, with the most amazing sand-bombs! It was great. We plastered the place from top to bottom. My two older sisters looked so ashamed of us when they were commanded to take us home.

"Ma... the twins are back early!"

I found things difficult at school, and I was slow at reading and writing. Yet I loved to learn. I was diagnosed with dyslexia later, but I was always frustrated with myself and convinced I was stupid. My twin Michael, on the other hand, took a lot of satisfaction from this. He was great with numbers, reading, and spelling, and often displayed a smarmy face in class. But Mum tried to encourage me from home by pointing out that I wasn't stupid since I strangely loved the *Encyclopaedia Britannica*. I pestered her to read things to me from them, particularly anything to do with animals, and I seemed to absorb and remember that information.

One thing I really loved about St Matthews school was my first teacher, Mrs Peterson. She was great. She took particular care in telling us about Jesus. I loved hearing about God, Jesus, Mary, and the apostles. She even took time to tell us dramatic stories about the early church martyrs who loved Jesus so much that they died for him. Through stories like these, she kindled such a love of God in my heart that I used to go home and find a place to pray, sometimes climbing trees to be alone and chat to God. I would then demand that God "make me a saint"! I used to get angry and disappointed when angels, like the ones I had noticed in our little prayer books, didn't show up on ethereal clouds to speak with me about God and commend me for my pious dedication.

During one of my prayer sessions, this time in the house, I looked out a crucifix. It had two large candle holders welded onto each side of it. Then, after rummaging in some of the kitchen drawers, I found two little birthday candles and some matches. When I put the candles into the oversized holders, they slid down, as they were far too small. I promptly lit them, and regrettably set my sisters' room on fire!

Unfortunately, my little pious life did not extend to the Mass. My brother and I hated going and thought it cold and boring. Every week, though, our paternal grandpa would faithfully come to pick us up and we would hide behind the couch, complaining, "We don't want to go, Ma!"

To this would always come the same response: "If you don't go, I'll have to take you to the Proddy church!"

Mum was from a Church of Scotland background, and although we had never been to a Protestant church, it was the "other side", and we were certain it must be much worse than Mass. After all, it was Protestant. This threat always prevailed, and Grandpa wouldn't have to beep the horn for too long before Michael and I would be sprinting toward the van. No way were we going to a "Proddy Church"!

When I was seven, my family moved into a large, detached, semi-rural house in Lasswade, about eight miles outside of Edinburgh. My dad seemed to have limitless entrepreneurial energy and endeavours. He had property and businesses all over the place, including several flats in Midlothian, along with a range of businesses from pubs to hair salons, as well as a director's box at Celtic's Parkhead. He had racehorses and greyhounds, and he paid for Mum to take flying lessons. As a family we would spend some summers in Florida at his house in Lakeland, and others in Ireland at the family's mountain cabin or village cottage.

Dad had come to Scotland from Ireland with his father at the age of eleven as a migrant worker to pick potatoes on the east coast of Scotland. Thankfully he never lost his earthiness, so amid his wide social network of friends and acquaintances there always remained the happy-go-lucky Irish man. Dad's business success created many exciting and privileged experiences as we grew up that gave us kids confidence in whatever setting we found ourselves. It was strangely normal for me to play football in a housing estate one day, then go shooting grouse on one of the finest moors in Scotland the next. At the weekends, when I wasn't hanging around the streets with mates, I was in Dunkeld in Perthshire receiving shooting lessons at the Stakis estate. Class distinctions just didn't exist for me back then. I happily enjoyed falconry with friends from Edinburgh's affluent Morningside as much as playing pitch and toss against the bookie's wall with my mates from the estate.

My dad, although strongly business-minded, never forgot to help others, and through him I was given my first practical examples of charity. Many times when travelling down the A1 to his contractor's base he would pick up men of the road, take them for a meal, and help them to the next stage of their journey.

Living in Midlothian could be pretty brutal. On one occasion, when I was about ten years old, I was heading to the shops on my rollerblades when two lads set about me. Ken and Iain, two older guys from one of the estates down the road, were drunk in the middle of the day and looking for trouble. As the blows kept coming at me, the first lad, Ken, salivating and screaming at me, took a brick and smashed it over my head. It caused a gash to open up and left a permanent scar on my skull. I never forgot this beating. With warm blood running down my face, I swore that one day I would get them back for this.

My brother also experienced similar violence in our area. Although definitely not a fighter, he was bright, confident, and extremely cheeky. He was usually able to keep other lads away with his ability to reduce most people to nothing with his acid tongue. He could humiliate and devastate other lads with just a few sentences. However, one day, while we were walking home from school, some lads grabbed him. It transpired that they had become sick of his talent for verbal deconstruction, and so these four lanky teenagers began to take turns attacking him. I just stood there, frozen with terror as these boys, who looked more like men in comparison to us, beat him. I was helpless, watching them as they laughed and asked each other, "Who wants another shot?" and repeatedly kicked him in the face. Michael kept looking at me with a confused and hurt expression, as I had not come to his aid.

"Please, I'm sorry, leave me," he repeated, but to no avail. They kept laying into him. I just stood there, shocked at their brutality. His whimpering cries were drowned out by the mockery and thuds of the older lads. Just when I thought they were going to leave him alone, they picked him up and kneed him repeatedly in the face. Then they let him fall to the pavement before they started all over again. Then one of the lads turned to me and sneered, "Do you want some too?"

"No," I stuttered in a feeble response.

Michael was now lying on the tarmac pavement, trembling. He had given up pleading with them to stop. "That's what you get for being cheeky," they jeered, concluding their assault by spitting on him.

I could not look my brother in the eye as I helped him home. The image of him lying helpless in the street, combined with the look of confused disappointment, only added to my cowardly shame.

That day affected me deeply. The attack, and the cowardice that had prevented me from jumping in for him, pierced my mind to the core. After that I started taking a weapon to school. I also made a conscious decision never to back down again. I would never allow myself to be bullied again, or see my friends or family given a hard time. No matter what! No matter what needed to be done. No matter what!

Michael and I were ten when Dad took us to a boxing gym a few miles up the road from our house. Undoubtedly, his intention was to toughen us up a bit. We entered the gym sheepishly, as the sounds of heavy thuds denting punchbags and whizzing skipping ropes screamed through the air. Someone shouted, "Come on, pick it up!" which served to incite further noise and vigorous activity from the men using the ropes.

"How are you doing, boys?"

A short, stocky individual spoke to us. He had a leathered and worn-looking face that looked battle-hardened and tough. His powerful shoulders were rounded so that even when he walked he appeared slightly hunched, as if always ready to duck a punch and respond with a counter. We had just watched this guy hitting the bag and his left hook looked as though it could have taken the head off a horse. We quickly jumped back behind our dad.

"Come on, don't be shy. This is my lad," the man said, pointing toward a menacing-looking boy with a shaved head, who looked about thirteen. He had well-defined muscles that stood out as he moved smoothly around the punchbag, hitting it with powerful flurries. As soon as I saw him, I thought to myself, *If I can be like him, nobody's going to batter me any more.*

"This is my son Greg, and my name's Grant," the man continued as we walked over to his son.

The tough-looking man speaking to us was Grant Ballantyne, an ex-professional boxer.

"Hiya," Greg said, briefly looking up from the bag, then returning to it with so much skill and coordination it made me think he hadn't even spoken.

I started to get excited about boxing. My eyes looked around the place, drinking in the sights of the speed balls being pounded rhythmically and guys hitting and dipping under the punch pads. My ecstasy was complete when Michael and I began sparring and it became apparent that, at boxing, he wasn't better than me. *Great!* I thought, *a legitimate way of beating my brother up – without any fear of parental reprisals.* Now I was the one with the smarmy face!

Michael was well liked by the men at the gym, who affectionately called him "Batman" on account of his unorthodox persistence in spinning round in the middle of a sparring session and trying to hit his opponent with the back of his hand. His style was more akin to Hollywood than the reality of the ring. He didn't stick at boxing long. He excelled at football instead, showing himself to be a good goalkeeper and eventually playing with the Celtic boys' club. My heart, however, was set on boxing and I began to eat, sleep, and breathe it. Even after tough sparring sessions with older lads that left me bleeding and crying, I always hungered for more.

When I turned eleven, the coach convinced my dad that it would be a good idea to lie about my age so I could start competing. The necessary paperwork was sorted out and I started fighting. I just found it strange that some of the lads I boxed had hairy armpits!

My sister Sinéad and I showed an interest in music, so Mum arranged for us to be tutored in Edinburgh by a man called Mr Pitblado. He offered guitar lessons from his house, but after only a couple of visits the lessons were cancelled for a while. Mr Pitblado's elderly mother, who he was living with, had passed away.

When we returned to continue our lessons, I overhead a conversation between my mother and Mr Pitblado. "Sorry to hear about your mother. How are you?" she asked.

How could anyone know that this simple conversation was about to shatter a kid's world?

"Not too good but getting on," he replied. "After all, we need to go on. No point giving up."

"I know, it's just so sad. Something like this can almost make you think, what is the point?"

Then, as if some dread bell had rung, ushering in a terrible malice, all of my attention turned sharply to humanity's common fate. I suddenly thought, *One day my ma will die, my da will die, I will die. If we are all going to die, what is the point? There is no point!*

I sank into a terrible depression that came over my mind like a black shroud, veiling everything.

By now, at the age of eleven, the faith that my primary teacher Mrs Peterson had kindled was forgotten. So dark and hopeless were my thoughts that my life became almost dreamlike. Everything appeared empty and unreal. Nobody seemed to be worrying about the things that bothered me; everyone else appeared to be content. It seemed insane to me that nobody was considering their fate and everything was just taken as a given: watching TV soaps, going for a jog, going to the pub.

What is the purpose? Everything is meaningless. They all have their stupid routines and it's all pointless. WHAT IS THE POINT? my mind screamed at me over and over again.

Now it was as if I was looking at life through a window from a cold outside. I felt hollow and forsaken by the rest of the world. It was like the feeling that remains in the pit of your stomach after you wake from a nightmare, except it underpinned all of my waking day. As I walked to school in the mornings I could hear the birds singing as if in mockery of me. Life was going on all around me. I thought about it, and envied the unconcerned creation. *Even the birds and animals can get on with their happy little lives.*

I wished I could just be "normal" again. Over and over I tried to reason myself out of this miserable state, only to reason myself back into it. I tried desperately to psych myself up for normal activities like going to school by trying to find some reason to go on...

Question: *Why should I go to school?*

Answer: *To do well, get good exams results, and become a wildlife vet. Then I'll get to Africa with the lions and stuff!*

Objection: *What's the point in that? I'm going to die, never mind the animals. Everyone I know and love will die. Like they say, one day the sun will explode, so even the ground I'm standing on will be gone.*

Conclusion: *It won't even be forgotten. There will be nothing and nobody to forget it. Things will be as if they never were. Pointless! Absolutely pointless!*

My mum would pick me up after boxing training or playing football and I'd sit in the back of the car, crying, unable to articulate fully the sense of impending doom I felt. "What are we here for?" "Why do we exist?" And always, "Why do we have to die?" were the questions I asked my parents.

My dad was quick to discourage such talk. "You're not right in the head. You'd better wise up, 'cause if you go on like this at your age you'll end up in the mental hospital." Little did he know I really felt I was losing my mind.

Desperate, I turned to my mum, who was growing more and more concerned. She would listen to my constant questions and try to help me by taking me into the countryside for long walks and drives. "Son, you must try to focus on the good and beautiful things in life."

I'd burst into tears. "Like what, Ma? Everything's pointless! We're going to die. The more beautiful things are, the worse is the sorrow for knowing it will pass. I have this feeling, this horrible feeling; it just won't go away. My stomach hurts with it." I was unable to communicate the depth of my depression. After all, I was too young to even understand what depression was.

Eventually I felt it was unfair to draw others any further into my interior misery, with my questions no one could answer. I feared others might enter this hell, so I carried my thoughts within. I then began to feel more and more isolated from people. I could not concentrate on anything. My parents noticed my lack of enthusiasm for everything – except boxing. This alone seemed to channel an unnatural amount of frustration, energy, and anger – something my trainers were quick to make use of. Mum, however, would try in vain to take me to a guitar lesson, or help me with my homework, or encourage my love for art. But I just could not will myself on any more. Emotionally, I felt like a corpse that someone was trying to resuscitate. Every morning I awoke in my bedroom next to my two brothers Michael and James, and I would hide my face in the covers and sob. I was devastated that the brief relief that my dreams and sleep had brought me was over and I had to get on with another pointless day.

Mum convinced Dad that I needed help. They thought travelling might broaden my horizons and lift my gloom. But it didn't. We went to Florida, Ireland, Egypt, Israel, Palestine, France, and many other beautiful places. I remember that Italy was particularly stunning. I was so privileged to see Venice, Florence, Rome, and Sorrento, but it didn't matter where I went, the despair was always there to greet me. Existence seemed an absolute tragedy. Nothing helped, and I sank deeper and deeper into this inner agony which infected everything. Despair accompanied me everywhere, consuming every last scrap of happiness, like a starving dog. No exterior beauty could lift this sense of meaninglessness. I would often have to quickly find somewhere private as the familiar feelings of panic and hopelessness would come over me again and again. Then I would just cry deep sobs which welled up from within. Why were things this way? Existence seemed an absolute tragedy.

So it was, and with this dark thinking my behaviour became darker.

After we returned home from school one day, a friend knocked at the door for Michael and me. It was Bryan, a lad who lived with foster parents down the road. He had spent most of his life in homes and secure units for unruly kids. My parents didn't know this, because he now lived in the affluent area along with us.

"Coming out?" he asked.

"Why not?" I replied, grabbing my coat and heading out the door.

We would just hang out and chat as we walked around the streets, speaking to girls from not far away. Michael and I were waiting for Bryan to return from a smooch with one of the local girls. I momentarily overcame my sinking feelings, which were being made worse by Bryan and Michael's carefree spirits. I asked my twin, "What's the point in life?"

By now Michael was getting fed up with my gloom, which he neither understood nor shared. "You're a weirdo. Life's for living." Quite content with his existential response, he said no more.

Just then, Bryan came running back to join us, laughing and out of breath. "If you kick the lamp post just right, it puts it out. Watch!" he laughed, and proceeded to kick the nearest lamp post in a forward stamping motion, right on the section used for entry into its wiring. BANG! Just like he said, the light went out.

We ran along the streets, kicking the lights out, with people beginning to shout and some giving chase. The excitement sent adrenaline coursing through my veins which, for the first time, caused me to forget my anguished thoughts.

Strangely, these actions were analogous to the change that was also taking place in my heart and mind. After that night, I started kicking out all the light that was left in my life. Everything became about living for that much-needed distraction, yet the hollow feelings remained. The motto "Life is for living" appeared to be the standard that most of the people I knew lived with. The pub, the football, the career, the money: everyone appeared to just do what they thought brought them "life" – or so I thought. Living for excitement became my pursuit, and a most welcome distraction. Whatever conscience I may have had became duller as I threw myself into all manner of mischievousness.

In high school, I began to hang around with lads from Danderhall on the outskirts of Edinburgh, and I was about twelve or thirteen when I started to drink with them at the weekends. Gradually, from these small towns on the edge of Edinburgh, my circle of friends and associates began to grow, like rings in a pond that grow wider and wider after a stone hits the surface, moving closer and closer to the city. I then started training in one of Edinburgh's roughest boxing gyms that was situated in the Craigmiller area. As my reputation for boxing grew, so too did my reputation for violence. The ring was not able to contain my inner turmoil.

I started fighting with other lads and groups of gangs across Edinburgh. Bare-knuckle scraps were organized up and down the city. I sought desperately to distract myself from the pain and pursued the "buzz".

At the age of fifteen, I was able to get into most nightclubs, as I looked much older than I was. I'd take wagers from my friends to see which bouncer standing at the nightclub door I could knock out with a single punch. Often this would go wrong, and after I'd smacked a bouncer I'd be picked up and tossed about like a rag doll. Yet even this was by far preferable to me than the inner agony.

The boxing training had by now become twisted into a means to gain a reputation, since I won many of the fights I became involved in. Many times I'd knock a person out during a fight and would just leave them unconscious, snoring on the cold pavement with their eyes still wide open. Images of men lying on the dance floor or pavement staring into space lingered long in my memory as the violence grew worse. The knots in my stomach that had accompanied the prospect of a fight in the early days had disappeared. Along with the "buzz" now came a crazed confidence and manic excitement.

Dad grew more and more concerned about his son who was losing it. On more than one occasion I heard him arguing with my mum because of my behaviour. "I HAVE SAID IT, THE POLICE HAVE SAID IT, THE SCHOOL HAVE SAID IT, THE PSYCHOLOGIST HAS SAID IT – HE'S NOT RIGHT IN THE HEAD!" It's unlikely they used Dad's words, but clearly people were talking. Dad would take me deer-stalking and game shooting all over Scotland, and during these weekend trips he would try desperately, in his own way, to talk with me about the trouble I was getting into. Whether it was the latest expulsion from school or Mum having to collect me in the middle of the night from a police station, he always tried to get me to stop and see how things were going to end up, and how different things might be if I would only change my behaviour. Yet I remained completely blinkered to the consequences of my actions, and refused reasonable advice from every quarter.

School became worse than ever. Now, having been kicked out of both St David's and Lasswade High School, I was meeting more regularly with the educational psychologist the school forced me to see. This didn't work. As I turned fifteen, I was sent to Gracemount High in Edinburgh, but they quickly made use of an exit strategy that allowed me to leave for "extended work experience". My behaviour was just intolerable. This was my third and final high school.

I took up an apprenticeship as a plumber with Dad's friend Gerald, and worked with Gerald's son, Paul. He was twenty-five at the time and, like his Dad, was an excellent plumber. However, he had a heroin problem, and it was while working with him that I first witnessed the drug. The sickly smell of smack running down the tinfoil as he "chased the dragon" became a daily spectacle for me during my working hours. I despised the drug but Paul continued to use it, and his addiction grew worse and worse. He died as a result of an overdose one year after I had started working with him.

I stayed away from drugs, mainly because of my commitment to boxing training. By the age of seventeen I had won the Scottish Eastern District and the Scottish Championship three times. I also won bronze in the Four Nations Championship (Ireland, Wales, England, Scotland). The ring was the only legitimate channel for my inner hell to be unleashed, and this caused me to succeed.

On one occasion I shared a venue with Amir Khan in

Bradford. During the fight at this venue, while boxing an English lad, my dark behaviour crept into the ring and I was disqualified. Nevertheless, later I went on to box for Scotland in Innsbruck, Austria.

The height of my boxing achievements came when, on 12 May 2002, I beat the British light-middleweight champion at a boxing show in Lesmahagow, and received the Best Boxer of 2002 award.

As my boxing career soared, life outside the ring descended deeper into darkness and violence. I was often reminded of a dream I had had as a child. It was a dream that always haunted me. I must have been about nine when I awoke from it screaming. Images of bloodshed, horrific violence, people in pain and distress, and terror made me leap from the bunk I was sharing with Michael and run crying into Mum's bedroom.

"I'm bad. I'm really, really bad," I wailed, crying and blinking through tears. She had my little brother James with her, who was bouncing joyously on top of the bed. She told me gently, "Calm down and just look into James' face. Can you not see his unconcern and happiness? Try, son, to be like him."

"But I've done terrible things," I kept repeating hysterically. "I'm bad. I'm so bad."

I had never had a nightmare like this, nor have I had one since. It felt so real.

2

Live by the Sword

"Tony, they're going to kill him! Get here!" screamed the voice down the phone, in desperation. It was a girl I knew.

"Who?" I asked. "Who are they going to kill?"

I could hear her crying and shouting, "KEV!"

She left the phone off the hook in her panic, and screams mixed with guttural groans howled down the receiver. She lived in Newtongrange, roughly four miles from where I was staying. I had no transport and no way of getting there. Filled with rage, I bolted out the front door, running into the night.

I hadn't even run a hundred yards when I noticed my brother's mate, Knoxy. His face was lit up by the light from his phone as he'd stopped his car to send a text message. I jumped into his front seat and demanded, "Get me to Nitten [Newtongrange] now!"

"What?"

"Move to Nitten!" I barked.

I was not in the mood for a refusal, and Knoxy understood it. He sped off, shock and concern etched into his already puzzled face.

I directed him to the girl's house and, as we arrived, I could see guys crossing backward and forward in the middle of the street. Kev and his mate Tam had been to a party and some of the local lads had turned on them. Eight lads were laying into the two of them, with delight. The car hadn't even stopped before I jumped out, took my belt off, and started running toward them.

"LET'S DO IT!" I shouted down the street.

The two who were nearest to me responded and began moving toward me. The others hadn't even noticed; they were too focused on kicking the face off Kev. I brought the heavy belt buckle across the first guy's face, and it broke immediately.

Meanwhile, Knoxy phoned my twin, Michael. "Your brother's a lunatic. He's just jumped into a gang of lads in Nitten, and there are loads of them."

"Is he getting done in?" asked Michael.

"No, well, eh, he's doing them and they're doing him."

"What does that mean?"

I had started fighting with the other lad, and it wasn't long before the rest of the gang noticed me. I was driven back to a fence by several of them but, as they tried to keep me pinned against it, I managed to wriggle my arms free and land several sickening blows. Shocked and surprised at this single-handed offensive, they continued to come at me. It was exhausting trying to keep myself up against the fence, although their punches were pathetically weak. Each lad gradually became more and more discouraged, through a mixture of tiredness and pain, as my punches rained onto their faces. After a while, they began to focus less on hitting me and more on keeping me held back. Like thieving poachers who had stepped on the spring of their own trap, they were now unable to go forward or backward without it snapping shut. They were stuck. Frothing at the mouth and panting heavily from a combination of fatigue and alcohol-induced dehydration, they were growing weaker and weaker.

Suddenly Kev, drunk and out of his face on drugs, jumped up from the pavement he had been lying on and ran at us. No punches, no kicks: he just ran. He was battered and cut, and unable to see through his swollen eyes – so he just went for everyone. His technique resembled more of a drunken stage dive than a combative manoeuvre, but he managed to knock the guys, himself, and me to the pavement. We all collapsed into an exhausted heap, with barely enough strength to get up and move off. The lads slowly dispersed, wheezing and coughing as they backed away down the street. However, one lad – not part of the original gang – strode menacingly toward me.

I jumped up and hit him square in the face with a crunching one-two!

Still he came forward.

I unleashed a five-punch combination – straight one-two-three-four left hook!

Still he kept coming.

I moved back and threw the best hook I had, followed by a brutal combination to his body and then his head.

Still he came forward!

I had nothing left.

My arms fell to my side as we walked into each other and began grappling, each trying to throw the other down. By now my body was utterly exhausted. I wanted to vomit. As we continued to wrestle, his head landed on my shoulder and so, with the last ounce of energy I had, I turned my neck and sank my teeth into his ear. I bit down hard into the tissue, then further again, and with a slight chew-jerk, ripped a chunk off his ear. He never moaned and never made a sound; we just moved slowly away from each other. The fight was over. I spat the bloody tatter of his ear to the grass and went home.

***

At the age of sixteen, I moved out of my parents' home and got a flat in Mayfield, Midlothian. I had grown tired of having to give account to my parents, and they were sick of my lifestyle. Every time Mum heard the whirr of the washing machine in the middle of the night, she wondered whose blood was being washed from my clothes. During the day I wore the cloak of an apprentice plumber, but by night I was involved in raids on shops, car thefts, drug deals, and credit card fraud. All of this was galvanized and reinforced by violence. My reputation for brutality had spread across the city like fire on a moor, and soon I was involved in a crime syndicate that spanned the entire city of Edinburgh. From Broomhouse to Niddrie, from the Inch to Royston, my mates and I were deeply committed to each other and to our one pursuit – making money.

At weekends we'd pick the horse racetrack we wanted to go to and call the ticket section. In my best Irish accent I would reserve "Owners and Trainers" badges using the name of an Irish millionaire and renowned racehorse owner. Then, wearing our tweed suits, we would demand our tickets like obnoxious folk from a rich retinue. With our false badges, people thought we owned or trained horses. It provided the perfect smokescreen for our fraud. Nobody batted an eyelid as we signed cheques for expensive paintings and clothing at stalls at the side of the track. Then, using £50 cheque guarantee cards, we'd make bets, always under £50, thus ensuring the cards would always clear. We placed so many bets that money was always made. We would even place bets on horses we knew to be non-runners, and then we would simply receive the cash back when we handed receipts in and state, "It never ran." It was bulletproof – they were giving us cash back for money that didn't exist. The track was a sweet swirl of champagne, laughter, and, as always, a welcome distraction.

Things didn't always go well. Many times I was caught off-guard leaving a pub or entering a house party. Often scenes erupted in the most unexpected ways, such as when I was at a house party in rough housing estate. A guy with a machete rang the doorbell to complain, "The music's too loud." I had maniacs try to stab, slash, run me over, set me up: you name it. This created a pervasive paranoia and made me suspicious of everyone.

So it was, one evening as I was leaving a pub on the edge of Edinburgh with several of my mates, a group of guys jumped out of a van and came after us with baseball bats. I stood my ground and smacked a lad to the pavement, but he clung to my legs and wouldn't let go. He held my feet together and kept me trapped. No amount of punches or eye gouges would make him release me. And through his immutable smirk he just kept repeating, "You're getting mangled when they get back. You're getting mashed."

He was referring to his mates with the baseball bats who were currently preoccupied with chasing my pals down the road, but they would soon return. Sure enough, in no time they were back. I watched as they came walking up the street, swinging their bats casually as they caught their breath. Catching sight of my predicament, they released ragged laughs and manic shouts of sheer delight. Seeing that they were nearly with us, I made one last attempt to free myself – I failed. In full anticipation of the brutality of the coming onslaught, I gripped my hands tightly round a nearby fence.

Then it started. Blow after blow rained down on the back of my head, causing my vision to blur. I brought one hand up to shield myself, tucking my head between my arm and shoulder and hunching my back up to cover as much of my head as possible. Those wielding the bats pummelled every inch of me, and it took all of my resolve not to uncover my head and instinctively place my hand where the pain was coming from. The aluminium bats made a distinctive "ping" when they missed and smacked the metal part of the fence that I was clinging to. The wooden bats, no matter what they hit – muscle, bone, flesh, or fence – made a thud like the sound of a body hitting the floor. Still I managed to keep myself up by holding on to the wire on the fence. Seeing this, they turned their attention to the hand I was desperately clinging on with. Like golfers teeing off, they took turns, smashing my hand with perfect accuracy until I could hold on no longer. I was still fully conscious when they threw me onto the middle of the road, smashing my skull and body with blow after blow. I curled up into a ball, expecting that I would wake up with a broken back or left permanently brain damaged like others I knew.

At that moment, the girl I was dating – Kim – came out of a nearby pub. She saw the attack taking place and, recognizing me as the victim, ran up the street screaming at the guys. It had no effect. Then, as I lay face down on the road, she fought her way through the group of attackers and lay on top of me, spreading herself out to protect me. This only infuriated them all the more and they began circling, picking off any limb not covered by her body. They just didn't give up. But then, all of a sudden, men and women came running down the street shouting, "Police! Stop!"

This finally sent the guys running into their van, and they sped off. It turned out that there weren't any CID at all, just a few brave people who thought that, if they didn't do something, they would witness a murder. Being saved by a girl and the local neighbourhood heroes was pretty humiliating!

This fight and others like it were part of a never-ending cycle in my life, but the scale and the consequences were starting to escalate to the point of no return. Like the night I received a telephone call from my mate Steve. "Tony, I've been done, mate," his voice sputtered down the phone.

He had been punched in the face by two local guys who had a reputation for bullying and intimidation. One of the guys had, without provocation, punched Steve so badly he needed stitches. This would be repaid. I told everybody who knew these guys that it was "on" between us. Things in the neighbourhood then began to escalate between "the young team" – my mates and me – and this group of guys in their late twenties and thirties – the "old team". Both gangs were made up of extremely tight-knit groups of guys, and loyalty was key. We would never have described ourselves as "gangs"; we were a bunch of mates who were in for each other. In reality, however, we were gangs.

So it began. One night I was out with my mates in a local pub when the old team came in. Immediately there was tension, but nothing kicked off. One of the old team came over and started swearing at some of my mates. I watched, infuriated as my friends just took it. I quickly shouted to the guy to get outside and he agreed to a square go. I walked out the door first, and as I went down the steps, he jumped on my back. This infuriated me, and I threw him off. We landed together on the pavement. I sprang to my feet first and, as he was getting up, I started kicking him in the face and stamping on his head.

Barely a few weeks later, when leaving another local pub, East Houses Miners Club, a car began to follow me, Greg, and another couple of mates as we walked home. It was clear that the old team were making a statement – they were watching us. Their car began to circle around us and then, as it came to do it again, I heard a smash as Greg threw a brick through their car window. In a flash they were out of their car and running toward us. We made toward them and, after some circling and posturing, we went for it.

A guy came for me. After a couple of digs, he fell to the ground. I stamped on his face and kicked him around the street. He curled up into a ball and I left him, turning to see Greg kneeling on a guy's chest and punching his head from left to right.

"I've called the police!" a woman shouted from her back garden across the street.

Greg and I made off quickly, as the guys we had been fighting began hurling threats and abuse in our direction.

"This isn't over!" they yelled. "You guys are dead!"

Between us and the "old team", it was well and truly on. I was now constantly in a heightened state of alert. Everywhere I went, I was ready. I didn't fear them, but I wanted to ensure that whenever the conflict came, the other person or people would be left severely damaged.

I always carried a brogue with me, a tool I used in my work which has a sharp spike for going through walls and testing for something to screw into. I would always be able to say, if I were caught, that I had left it in my pocket after work and thus would be less likely to be charged. However, if I was jumped or set upon, my full intention was to use this to stab anyone who tried to attack.

Early one morning, I was up for work and heard footsteps bounding up the stairs. Immediately my English Bull Terrier began to grunt and bark. I looked through the spy hole and noticed two brothers from the old team standing there but looking hesitant, because of the barking. I never gave them a chance to think: I grabbed my spike and jumped out with one hand in my pocket and the other holding back the snarling Bull Terrier. They turned white.

"What do you want?" I shouted, my voice echoing down the stairwell.

They began to stutter and stammer, "Tony, you can't do this."

"Do what?" I demanded, gripping the dog's chain as he strained to get at them.

"You can't go about doing people in," they replied, referring to the incident a few nights ago, when Greg and I had been followed and subsequently had smashed the car and given the old team a beating.

"I don't care. Your mates are bams and were easy," I shouted. "In fact, let's go down the stairs – you two and me – and sort this."

They began to shuffle uncomfortably, protesting about how they had really come with peaceful intentions. I was nobody's fool. Their steel toe-capped boots and padded gloves indicated that they had come early with the intention to catch me off guard, but had subsequently received a sharp shock.

I increased my threats toward the two brothers, sending fear among the others in Mayfield. Though I attempted to arrange some "square goes" through friends of theirs, it was to no avail. They, on the other hand, while continuing to avoid me, continued to insult me.

Then one afternoon I received a phone call. "They're in the MFI (Mayfield Inn), loads of them, and they're telling you to come ahead."

I called Greg and we picked up a side-by-side double-barrelled shotgun and headed up to meet them. We were fully armed and ready for a fight. My earlier shooting lessons had taught me not only how to shoot, but also where and when gamekeepers left their guns unattended. After big shooting days, Land Rovers and Jeeps were often unlocked and unobserved as everyone headed to a countryside pub to celebrate their 200 bird day and reminisce about their fine shots. Shotguns were an easy grab.

On the way to the pub, Greg pulled out frantically in front of another car. When the guy in the other car began hurling abuse at us, I jumped out and began fighting with him. It was insane. Here I was fighting in the middle of an extremely busy road, cars whizzing by, all the while running the risk of being found with a double-barrelled shotgun and cartridges in the car. Suddenly Greg "Judased" him (attacked him unexpectedly and in an underhand way) and knocked him out. We quickly pushed him inside his car – still unconscious – and closed the door.

By the time we got to the pub, several of the guys, including the brothers, were heading down to another club just down the road. We stopped the car and jumped out. As soon as they laid eyes on the shotgun, the old team disappeared, swearing and scampering away. The guys we had come for bolted through gardens, sending washing lines up through the air and articles of clothing flying in their train.

Rumours later came back: "They're saying you had a gun that could've killed a dinosaur!"

I felt that a sufficient warning had been issued by this incident.

I was wrong.

***

"Tony, he's just smacked him again and split his stitches wide open."

My mate informed me that one of the brothers had burst Steve's face open again. After all the warnings, threats, and fights this had caused, he had blatantly done it again!

By now my flat was under constant police surveillance. The gun incident had attracted their attention like nothing on earth. Police cars and vans had taken to sitting outside my flat all the time; they even had a dog section prepared for my dog. It was clear they seriously wanted me off the street.

Then it happened. As Greg and I entered the Mayfield Inn, a man jumped up and began staring at me. It was one of the brothers I was looking for. I walked over to his table, looked him straight in the eye, and ordered, "Get outside."

He made no response except to smile and sit down.

"Get yourself outside, you idiot."

He just sat there at the table that separated us. I headed to another table and sat down, planning my next move.

He then picked up his phone and I could hear him calling his people, saying, "They're here."

I knew immediately that he was calling others to the pub. We were sitting ducks. Greg and I quickly jumped into a taxi and made to a house. We collected two samurai swords and concealed them before jumping back into the taxi and telling the driver, "Back to the pub."

Keeping the weapons hidden as we passed the pub, we could see four men heading in the direction of my flat. We overtook them in the taxi without them noticing, and moved further down the street without being seen. We got out of the taxi and carefully made our way through a dark car park that gave way to a lane, through which we could pass unseen and cut the men off at the end of the road. We walked out onto the main street in Mayfield.

"Let's do it," I said.

Greg and I looked at each other and grinned.

"Come on then, let's go!" yelled Greg.

We unsheathed our swords and walked toward them. The two men accompanying the brothers spotted the weapons and immediately ran off. The two brothers, having been out drinking since earlier that day, ran straight toward us. Greg went for one and I went for the other.

One of them rushed toward me and I brought the blade down, slicing it across his chest. He froze with terror. I then swung the blade around, slashing the side of his skull. As he fell to the ground and tried to protect himself with his hands, I slashed the blade down again forcefully. With blood oozing out of every injury, he collapsed onto the road, and Greg and I chased his brother up the street.

3

On the Run

"OPEN THIS DOOR OR WE'LL SMASH IT DOWN!"

The shouts of the CID filled the stairway to Greg's flat, with many more uniformed officers behind them spilling out into the street. The door burst open and an army of them rushed in.

"Hands against the wall!" they shouted. Seeing no escape, we promptly followed their orders, recognizing that retaliation or the use of force would be futile. Our arms were handcuffed behind our backs, we were sat down on the furniture in Greg's living room, and our rights were read to us. A large, fair-haired CID officer with dark eyes and a serious face began to ask me my name and date of birth.

"What is your occupation?" The officer asked.

I mocked him.

Then, looking at me with an expression that was both puzzled and angry, he responded, "Let's get them to the station."

We were arrested and charged with attempted murder. In the police station we were shown what the police had recovered – two blood-spattered swords. After the fight the night before, Greg and I had handed them to a friend and told him to get rid of them. His face had fallen in horror, aghast at what he knew we had done. Trembling, he had taken the swords and had disappeared into the night. It turned out that in his fear he had almost immediately shoved them into a skip not far from the scene of the crime. A police dog had picked up the scent and they had been recovered at once.

We were remanded in custody at Edinburgh Sheriff Court and taken to HMP Edinburgh (Saughton), and from there we were taken to Glenesk where remand prisoners are held. I did not intend to stay there long, so I quickly began making arrangements to get money to my lawyer so he could get me High Court bail. Even the legal system of Scotland, with all its judicial pomp and ceremony, is subject to monetary manipulation.

Two weeks later, an officer banged on my cell door and informed me that I had been granted bail. Now free, and anticipating a High Court trial in a few months for attempted murder, I quickly set about finding out who the witnesses were and "putting things in order", which really meant using threats and intimidation in an effort to secure a favourable verdict. I was certain that this would sort things out sufficiently, and confident that I would not be going to prison for long.

Meanwhile, I took up where I had left off and threw myself into the same criminal activities as before. Things were as busy as ever. By now, my friends and I had connections not only in Edinburgh but in Glasgow too. Money was easily made and there was no looking back. Life became a surreal haze; the "real world" of work, routine, order, and predictability was gone. From one day to the next, I lived on the edge and welcomed any crisis as an opportunity to advance in both reputation and status.

So it happened as I was driving around with my mates in a vehicle that had been used repeatedly for smash and grabs, a police car drove past us. Seconds later I noticed in the rear-view mirror that they were turning and had switched their blue lights on. It was one week before my driving test – a massive deal when you're seventeen. To stop would mean an immediate ban, not even to mention the connection to all sorts of robberies, so I put my foot to the floor. The police Volvo T5 was far quicker than the old battered Renault I was driving. Nevertheless, I was determined not to stop – after all, I was still on High Court bail. To be stopped would mean no driving licence and immediate imprisonment. So with this in mind, the blue lights hotly pursued us through the streets, back roads, and highways of Edinburgh. My car was packed with mates all shouting directions as I weaved in and out of the streets, speeding through give-ways and stop signs in the dead of night. We passed through badly lit areas and drove onto grass embankments, cutting through parks and dodging the council's "No Ball Games" signs. Every time I thought we had lost them, they would appear behind us.

"They're well up for it," the lads laughed.

Soon we noticed another police car behind us; there were now two cars chasing us. I flew into an Edinburgh road scheme known as "The Inch", knowing that we could enter and exit the scheme swiftly with some hard-to-follow turns. I hoped to round several corners quickly enough to lose them and get onto the faster road that led away from the estate. We shot through the scheme, bits of car flying off as we bounced over what seemed like an endless terrain of speed bumps.

As we pulled out of The Inch we picked up speed, but coming round a corner I spotted a traffic police car waiting for us on the road ahead. An officer was standing at the back of his car, wildly waving his arms in the air in a vain effort to make us stop. With no intention of doing so, I flashed my lights mockingly at him as I overtook his car. In the rear-view mirror I saw him sprinting to his car to join the pursuit.

We now had three police cars chasing us as we snaked in and out of the city. We were not losing them, and soon we would have to jump out and run. Then, to my horror, I heard a cry from the back seat: "The dogs, man. They've got the dogs!"

I looked in the mirror and saw the dreaded white van joining the convoy; it was the police dog section. "Not the mutts!"

The voices from the back seat lost their humour completely; we were all too familiar with horror stories of mates being caught by the dog squad. Some of them still bore ugly reminders of the event – ragged scars covering arms and thighs, the result of being pulled down and brutally savaged. We had to think fast about how and where we could jump out of the car.

"GUYS, WHERE CAN WE GO? IT HAS TO BE CLOSE TO A HOUSE WE CAN REACH FAST!" I yelled.

"Or at least close to a tree we can climb," said Martin.

"We can't even stab them. They class it as stabbing an officer," yelled Chaz.

Sparko cut in, "There's an alleyway at the back of my house. We can run through. If we're quick enough, we'll get through it and they won't see where we've gone." Sparko was bright and often right.

"That's back at The Inch," I said, knowing it was our only chance. With four police vehicles desperately trying to catch us and undoubtedly more on the way, I faced the problematic task of somehow finding a way to turn round and get back to The Inch – in spite of these pursuers! Fortunately for us all, we knew Edinburgh like the back of our hands, and it wasn't long before we'd completed a weaving U-turn across the city in the direction of Sparko's house.

As we flew into the estate, seat belts began popping inside the car as we anticipated the swift exit and speedy bolt we would need to make down the path. Chaz, a very small lad, had even opened the sunroof, as he was in the back middle seat – no valuable seconds could be wasted.

The road Sparko had in mind led to a cul-de-sac with a long alley at the end. As we sped down the dead-end road, I jammed the car into second gear and, with a great jolt and scream from the engine, our speed reduced dramatically. Car doors swung open as my mates bailed out before it had even stopped.

I jumped out and started running. Glancing behind, I could see the car mounting the pavement and rolling into the communal rose bushes, as Chaz desperately tried to pick the right moment to leap from the sunroof. It wasn't long before he was running too. As we legged it through the pitch black alley, we heard the sound of police cars screeching to a halt and doors banging. Suddenly, screams pierced the night. The terrible ear-splitting, stomach-churning screams of somebody being mauled by a dog added fresh speed to our legs. Someone had been caught…

Our footsteps clattered heavily up the stairs into Sparko's attic, waking his parents. They began shouting at us and demanding an explanation. We left it to Sparko to give one. The rest of us opened up the attic roof window and peered down at the scheme through which we had made our hasty escape. The dog had got someone, but who? We did a quick head count, but we were all there. Every one of us had made it to the attic. But someone had been mauled. From our hidden vantage point we could see the police searching every street and garden in a vain attempt to find us. The search was thorough and they were determined, but we were safe.

It wasn't until the next day that we heard what had happened and who the unlucky victim had been. When we jumped out of the car and sprinted down the alley, the police officers closest behind us came after us on foot. However, when the dog section arrived and let the dog off the lead, it shot off after our pursuers and took down the nearest officer in the pitch black alley.

***

Satisfied that everything was now in order concerning those who would dare to give evidence against me at my approaching trial, I decided to hand myself in to the police. They had issued warrants for my arrest, owing to my growing criminal activities. It wasn't for the car chase, but for other criminal activities that they were pursuing me, and they had been going through home after home only to find that I continually eluded them.

One evening I decided to hand myself in at the local police station in Bonnyrigg. It was a little police station on the outskirts of Edinburgh, and a young female officer was on duty who did not know me. She reported my appearance to headquarters in Dalkeith and to her surprise, within seconds of putting down the phone she was called back. I could see that there was a serious conversation going on. Within minutes, police cars rushed to the small police station and I was taken to headquarters in Dalkeith in Midlothian.

Unknown to the officers, before handing myself in I had put almost half an ounce of cannabis into a yoghurt and had eaten it. (Tumbling further and further down the rabbit hole, I now had no issue with drugs.) Its effects on me soon began to be obvious. I was standing with the officers as they itemized my belongings, and I started to giggle. The team of officers around me seemed so comical. They were astonished, convinced that they were dealing with a maniac. After they had put my belongings into a box marked "Gielty", I noticed they did not hand my belt back to me.

"Afraid I'm going to hang myself, are you?"

"Hanging would be too good for you. We've got better plans for you," replied a powerfully built officer. I could not help but laugh at his self-assurance.

After this, it wasn't long before Greg and I were scheduled to appear at Edinburgh High Court. Because of fear of witness intimidation, the judge, Lord Hardy, had ordered a "closed court", meaning the trial would not be open to the public.

The trial was over after three days. Some of the witnesses did not point us out, much to the confusion of the procurator, a tall, thin, upright young man with dark hair who wore thick-rimmed glasses. They had already told the police they knew us and could point us out again. Unknown to the procurator, these witnesses understood, through a discussion with a person unknown, that in Scottish law it is not a crime to say later in court that what they formerly told police was "untrue", provided they reveal "the whole truth" in court. Despite the confusion and doubt the witnesses brought to court, however, the DNA found on the swords proved beyond reasonable doubt that we were guilty. Lord Hardy postponed sentencing for a period of three weeks to review background reports.

HMP Edinburgh (Saughton)

Meanwhile, these weeks in prison in Saughton were spent in solitary. Earlier, Greg had been taken to the segregation unit for fighting and, not wanting him to be alone, I thought I would do something to ensure I could, in some way, keep my friend company. In solitary, prisoners can speak to each other out of the windows and from under the cell doors. I therefore decided one evening to smash up my cell, to break anything and everything that could be broken. I started by ripping the sink off the wall, causing water to rush up through broken pipes, flooding my cell and gushing out under my door on to the wing. I then proceeded to break the prison furniture to pieces, realizing that the steel chair legs would provide me with substantial weapons for when the "MUFTI mob" came.

When I was finished, the cell was completely trashed. While smashing it up, I had been frequently interrupted by loud bangs on the door. The spy-hole would be opened from the outside and a few prison officers would breathe threats and warn me to stop. I responded with my own threats and a torrent of abuse, causing the other prisoners on the wing to cheer. This enraged the officers all the more.

After a few hours on my own, soaking wet and, to be honest, a bit bored of it all, I heard the yell of several voices, "Get your hands against the back wall now!"

I responded by swearing and telling the officers that they would regret coming into the cell. Unknown to them, I had taken my prison-issue shampoo and poured it all out in front of the cell door. My intention was to make sure that the first few riot officers slipped and fell as they came in, allowing me to attack them with my steel chair leg. Sure enough, the door was flung open and my temporary barricade, which I had thought pretty well constructed, was demolished in seconds. I had not foreseen that, at times like these when barricades are used, the cell door can be opened from the other direction. "Misdemeanours" such as these are common in prisons, and officers are well schooled in combatting them. However, they had not anticipated my second line of defence. As they ran toward me with shields and batons raised, the first officer slipped on the shampoo and fell to the ground, causing the second to tumble over him. I sprang up and began to smash them over the head with the chair leg.

The entire situation was comical. They had robust helmets which prevented them from coming to any harm, yet they hadn't prepared for the slippery surface and struggled to manoeuvre their bodies and shields into an upright position. Nevertheless, after what felt like ages, but can't have been more than ten minutes of sliding about in soapy bubbles trying to regain control, more prison officers entered. In no time, my face was smashed on the floor, and my eyebrow opened up badly as several angry blows of reprisal rained down upon me. I was put into an arm lock and marched forward, my head facing the floor and my back painfully arched. The coarse gloves the prison officers wore were so rough that, at random points when they grabbed me by the face, it felt as though my skin was being ripped off. I was marched into my solitary cell and, held down by the prison officers, patched up by the nurse. The chaos and excitement of the adrenaline-fuelled frenzy was over.

Soon the officers and the nurse left. I was on my own now, my first night in solitary. I had achieved my goal, to be there for Greg, but had I known what I would go through in this initial visit to solitary I would have reconsidered, as I entered one of the darkest periods of my life. Suddenly, out of nowhere, I experienced torturous inner thoughts and memories that haunted me. Within those walls I found it impossible to distract myself. With those dark thoughts and memories tormenting me, the biggest struggles in solitary were the interior battles of mind and heart. I found myself unable to sleep for days and nights on end. It wasn't the anticipation of spending years in prison, nor was it fear for my own safety. Rather, anxiety and restlessness made their home within me, as my mind continually reflected on the way I had lived my life, sickening me through its constant dredging up of the terrible things I had done. Guilt and shame consumed me.

Trying to eat amid so much anxiety was all but impossible: my nerves were shattered. I could not escape; there were no distractions, and nowhere to run from myself. As my own heart and conscience continually reproached me, I began to truly hate myself. I can recall trying to pick up a pen to write to my family and being filled with such shame of myself that I determined they could not possibly love me. Or if they did, then it must be because they did not really know me. Such was the extent of my inward darkness and pain that I became utterly convinced this was true.

In solitary, the weight of my torments increased to such an extent that all I wished for was to die. I felt I was staring into the abyss of my soul and it reflected nothing back but treachery and the deepest inclinations toward evil. Thoughts of suicide were my closest companions in that place and, though I could never have brought myself to do it, I desperately wanted to die. Thoroughly convinced that there was no hope for me, I determined, right there and then, that I would fully resign myself to my vileness, giving full vent to my inward evil. It was as if a darkness had revealed my hidden darkness in order to create more darkness.

On 31 October 2003 I was taken to Kilmarnock High Court and given a ten-year prison sentence. My best friend and co-accused, Greg, was sentenced to twelve years. Greg had already served time for violence and so received a heavier sentence; I received a lesser sentence because this was my first time in prison. After we returned from the High Court, and our handcuffs were taken off and we were placed back into our respective solitary cells, one of the screws commented on our cell numbering. He pointed out, to Greg's and my astonishment, that the whole time we had been awaiting our sentences, we had been in cells that reflected the sentences we would receive: I was in cell number ten and received ten years; Greg was in cell twelve and received twelve years. A strange coincidence?

4

Abandon All Hope, You Who Enter Here

HMYOI Polmont

HM Inspectorate Report HMYOI Polmont 2004, Nevis Hall:

2.10 Nevis holds what are known locally as "non-conformists". These are young adults who have been downgraded from the mainstream convicted population because of their behaviour in general or after specific incidences of violence, bullying or misbehaviour. However, no attempts are made to deal with or challenge their behaviour while in Nevis. The atmosphere in the hall is tense and oppressive, and a serious incident had taken place in the exercise yard a couple of weeks before the inspection.

2.11 In "A" section, 10 prisoners are held on a very limited regime. The night sanitation is switched off and the prisoners have to "slop out". They have EPIC but no television, kettle or lamp. There is little opportunity for activity outwith the hall. The staff described this section as the "assessment" section but some prisoners were working their way back into mainstream after a period in segregation. The facilities in this section were poor, and while permission would also have to be sought from SPS HQ to keep young adults in the Segregation Unit on Rule 80, no such permission is required for "A" Section in Nevis. To all intents and purposes the prisoners in "A" section are out of association.

2.12 There are four showers in metal cubicles, for the whole hall. There is graffiti on many of the cell walls, food is served from a cupboard in the centre of the hall and prisoners take their meals back to their cells to eat. The facilities for dishwashing are not good. Plates and cutlery are collected after use and washed in a cupboard at the end of one of the sections. This practice should stop and the facilities generally should be improved.[1]

"Abandon all hope you who enter here" only applies to the person who has hope left to abandon. This place would become the canvas on which I would paint pain, using other people as my palette and their blood for my signature.

We were taken straight to Nevis, where the all-star team of "non-conformists" was kept. As we approached the final grille before entering the place, the hall pulsed and throbbed with hatred. This place contained the worst of the worst. People from all over Scotland would be dragged here after being booted out of the mainstream prison population. Indeed, Nevis "shone" as a beacon of innovation and forward thinking in prisoner reform.

We were taken to our cells in A-section. The corridors were dark and oppressive, as if they watched you as you walked, frowning and lurching, waiting to chew you up and spit you out like thousands before you.

As soon as the cell door closed behind me, I wanted to vomit. The prisoners the day before had staged a "dirty protest". Clearly my cell had been used in this and was filthy. Such protests involve prisoners taking their own excrement and smearing it on the walls. My cell had not been cleaned properly from the day before and on the walls there remained the encrusted remnants of the previous prisoner's faeces. The smell was suffocating, and I was made to eat in this filthy cell. I went to open the window of my cell and banged it with my fist in frustration as I realized it would only open an inch.

Disgusting protests like these happen when human beings are driven to despair through dehumanizing treatment. The soul forgets its dignity and decency in a desperate attempt to protest against the injustice it is subjected to. Subhuman actions often occur within subhuman environments. But in the end, everyone suffers.

A-section was a corridor within Nevis itself that was far worse than solitary. In the digger, at least we had a toilet. Here we just had a pot, which filled up quickly because of the amount of hours we were locked up alone. We were forced to throw our bodily waste out of the windows. My cell was on the ground floor of the wing, so everyone else's waste from above was right outside the window. I had never seen such a dehumanizing environment.

I was given solitary exercise, which had to be taken first thing in the morning. I had arrived in November, so it was pitch black outside for my exercise session. Yet blacker still was my thinking. My days were spent absorbed in my interior world of pain. At night I would lie awake, listening to the other prisoners talking and shouting out of their windows. Yet something in the hardship of Nevis produced a humour among the lads that kept them laughing.

"Alright, son." Three burly screws were standing at the door to my tiny cell. "We've heard about your carry-on in Edinburgh, so know this: we won't be taking any of it in here."

The one speaking apparently had a very matter-of-fact way of communicating. I decided to respond in kind. "Well, boss, thanks for the fresh start. Do me a favour and get lost!"

"We'll see," they growled, slamming the door shut.

I'd heard the groans of other YOs (young offenders) as screws opened their cells at unexpected times and attacked them. Their classic approach was simply to tell a lad that they were "strip-searching" him. Then, as the unsuspecting YO pulled his top over his head to undress, they would punch him in the stomach, winding him. Then they would all jump on him and cart him off to the digger. "Carting" has the guise of legitimate restraint. It involves each officer going for a limb, then tackling the prisoner to the ground. The wrists are bent backward into an L-shape and the person is then made to stand up, but is arched forward with his head facing the ground. Any resistance is felt at the point of most pressure – the wrists. While it is certain that prisoners need to be restrained, it is unacceptable when wrists are snapped in the process: the amount of times YOs seemed to "injure themselves" while being restrained was remarkable. It seemed that extraordinary feats of "self-harm" were possible: swift kicks to the head, body, and legs could all be expected during a cart from Nevis screws.

***

"Pack it up, you're moving."

I was seventeen. There was a hall for YOs between the ages of 16 and 18, called Lomond. I arrived in Lomond just before dinner time, and we had to walk from our sections through the long corridors down into the dining hall. On the way down I could hear Glaswegian accents shouting and asking who I was.

But they knew, since newspaper headlines about a "brutal boxer" who had been involved in "a cruel samurai attack" had been plastered on the tabloids. Contrary to reason, rather than this making me someone to be avoided, I was now a target. To attack a boxer would enlarge anyone's reputation and so, even on my arrival, the shouts, taunts, and challenges began.

In the dining hall, an Edinburgh lad showed me where I was to sit. Everyone followed this unwritten code of conduct, and I was to sit with those from my area.

"They're on top, like," said a thin, weaselly looking lad from Edinburgh's Leith area, subtly gesturing in the direction of a large group that made up most of the dining hall. "The weegies, man."

"Aye, they've got the place right underhand," said another lad, Paul. It was clear to me that they were very, very afraid.

"Best to keep the head down, Tony," advised the lad from Leith.

"I'll do my own time, pal," I snapped.

The group of lads they had just described resembled nothing less than a bunch of young chimps getting excited at feeding time. They high-fived each other, made silly noises, and stood out in sharp contrast to the rest of the hall, which sat quietly, each lad staring intently at his table. The Aberdeen table, as well as the Dundee one, hardly spoke, while the Glasgow table had a great time, each lad trying to outdo the other in banter and jokes. A very large group of imbeciles had managed to take over the wing.

I chuckled to myself.

"What you laughing at, T?" Paul asked.

"This whole set-up," I replied.

"Eh?" He looked at me quizzically.

"It's so funny." As we walked back up to the wing from the dining hall, one guy rushed past me, then another, and still another. Davie, who was walking with me, just sighed deeply.

"What's up with you?" I asked.

"Look," he said.

I stuck my head out of the long line of green tops marching along the corridor like mindless zombies heading back to their graves. There was a commotion happening some thirty metres ahead of me. I could see people just walking by as the group of guys took turns stabbing their pens into a young lad's face. Like mongrels snapping and biting, they circled and harassed. They were brave in numbers, but I could see that, like whinging scavengers, they were utterly incapable of standing on their own. I noticed that the YO being "done in" was from Edinburgh, since he had been at my table during dinner. Yet all the Edinburgh boys just kept walking past him with their heads down.

I ran forward and rushed at the group of guys. I hit one of them with a straight right hand, which knocked him to the floor. Without a thought I pivoted, swinging my body round to bring a crunching left hook into the face of another. In no time there was a swarm of people flying at me, but they rushed at me, swinging their arms like forward-facing windmills. In the boxing ring, we would call people who fought like that "swimmers", because they looked like they were doing a front crawl. They were wide open for ferocious upper cuts, which rocked them. There was a sickening look on their faces as they wondered why their legs betrayed them and sent them to the ground or into directions undesired. After I had knocked another two to the ground, the first lad got up and kicked me. I headbutted him and burst his face open. Other guys from Glasgow came to put the boot in, but I taunted them as they hit me: in the gym I'd received much worse than this just in sparring sessions. Now and again I would get free enough to land a good connection on a punch.

Then suddenly, I was grabbed from behind in a chokehold by a screw, while another took my legs. They had started taking me away when one of the Glasgow boys ran and kicked me while I was being held back. Somehow I managed to get away from the screws and started running over to the chimp who had kicked me. He just stood there, shocked that I was now free. Curling himself up into a ball, he received my retaliation. I'm convinced the screws let me go after they saw him taking the liberty of hitting me while I was held back.

The screws dragged me back to my cell and slammed the door behind me, and the whole wing went into uproar. The YOs flocked to their windows to speak to each other and swear their allegiance to the Glasgow boys. Threats were shouted at me from what seemed like every window in the jail. I paced back and forth. I'd have to put a razor together, sharpen a dagger, make sure my kettle was boiled for as soon as the doors opened.

Just then, keys clashed against the door and it flew open. "Do you want to move?" said a screw, standing there expectantly, with two others behind him.

"Nope," I replied.

"If you stay here, you're going to get killed." There was no danger of me going on protection. That was for the lowest of the low, and I refused to be a coward. I would rather be killed.

"Leave me alone."

"You're going to get done in, son. Think about it."

"Bring it on! " I shouted. "I'm not afraid of anyone, especially not a bunch of starving vermin! Let them come!"

I could hear the YOs all across the jail now, as they began to shout backward and forward. My silence only reinforced their bravado.

"Here you, ya dafty, get to your window," they hollered.

"Listen up," continued another. "You're getting slashed to bits."

Each of their pithy statements was followed by a huge cheer. I kept silent as their threats continued.

"I'm taking an eye clean out of your head," another bellowed amid the uproar.

Torrents of abuse were hurled at me, reinforced by the crudest threats pertaining to every inch of my anatomy.

I noticed some mail from my family sitting next to the sink in my cell. I sat down for a moment while the cursing, roaring, and door-banging continued. I dreaded receiving mail from my family and loved ones. I wanted to disappear. I just wished I could be forgotten, never to be contacted or seen again. I wanted to forget everyone so much: their love and concern only added to my pain and shame. I felt it was all false. It was easier to hate and be hated than receive love. *Nobody could love or care about me anyway, if they truly knew who I am, or the things I've done*, I thought.

Day after day since the start of my sentence a battle had raged within me. The exterior battle that was about to take place was nowhere near as ugly as the inward battles being fought. Self-hatred coursed through my veins with every heartbeat, poisoning all positivity. Always I felt the continual pull into the abyss of my soul, which brought fresh regrets of evil deeds that haunted me. I wanted to die so much, but suicide just wasn't an option – it would be too easy. Rather, I fantasized about running into a gang and having a lock-back stuck in my lung, or a screwdriver through the skull, or a razor opening my neck. I longed for death to end this living hell.

As the screws did their final count before leaving that night, I was still on lockdown because of the fight earlier that day. Because I had not been to my window to defend myself before the onslaught of window warriors, this was taken as a sign that I was afraid. The threats continued into the night, until finally I had had enough.

"MY NAME'S TONY GIELTY, 80585, FROM EDINBURGH!" I screamed with everything inside me.

"Lomond F section, first cell on the right. First thing in the morning I'll make my way to the can [communal toilet], and let anyone that wants to come ahead, be there. I am coming for you! You better hope you kill me, because if you don't, I'm tooled to the back teeth and I'm not wasting my time with punching you about again. This time I'm burying you. The ones I leave alive will have to pick their guts up in a wheelbarrow and run to the surgery to pick up the bags they'll be carrying about for the rest of their days." Then, to finish this explosion of abuse, I roared, "YAAAAAASSSSSS! WHOOOOHOOOO! HERE'S TONY, YOU DIRTY RATS!"

Absolute silence followed my outburst. Then sounds of cells being smashed to pieces could be heard all over the wing, as prisoners attempted to get moved before the morning.

Throughout the night I prepared myself by reinforcing the thick plastic forks and knives that could be sharpened into a sharp solid spike. I melted two razor blades (that I'd managed to keep within my waistband) into the end of my toothbrush, to make a "double-whammy". This is a commonly used weapon in prisons, where two razor blades are placed side by side in order to make it as difficult as possible to stitch the slash it creates. In the effort to sew the slash made by one razor, the skin is ripped away from the other wound made by the adjacent razor. I looked out my pot and some sugar: I'd fill the pot with boiling water from the kettle then pour the sugar into it. This would mean I could scald a person severely, as the boiling water mixed with sugar melted onto their skin.

My odds were not good, but I was going out in style. I paced back and forth all night, ready and waiting for whatever was coming at me in the morning.

I heard the sound of keys opening the door to my cell. "Right, you're going to see the unit manager [wing governor]," said the supervising officer, a powerful-looking man with a whole squad of white shirts behind him.

I was taken into a large room with a big table. At the other end sat a grey-haired man in a pristine suit, with two other supervising officers next to him.

"You've managed to rid my hall in a single night of our main bullies. In an ideal world I'd give you a medal," he stated.

What does he mean, rid the hall of the main bullies? I thought to myself.

"Eh?" I said, looking at him for an explanation.

"Your friends have smashed up their cells to get away from you," he replied. "Three days solitary. Dismissed."

HM Inspectorate Report concerning HMYOI Polmont 2004, Dunedin [solitary] Unit

2.28 Those prisoners on punishment are not given a radio and their bedding is removed from their cell between 7am and 5pm. This is a practice that stopped in adult establishments many years ago. Polmont should review the way young adults in cellular confinement are treated.[2]

These guys had smashed up their cells to get away from me but were taken straight to the downgrade hall, Nevis, which I had not long left. Thinking they were in a safe place, they started talking back and forth to each other about how they were going to exact revenge on the "insane boxer" back in Lomond. Unfortunately for them, my best friend Greg could hear every word from within another section, since he was still contained in Nevis. Greg was a go-ahead, in the truest sense of the word. I had never known him to be afraid or back down. He carried with him an infectious confidence, which he was able to impart to those closest to him, giving courage and strength to his friends. He was a natural leader. I had boxed for Scotland at an international level, but Greg had always outclassed me in the ring. These lads were well and truly out of the frying pan and into the fire.

"Hey you, that's my co-accused you're talking about. Make sure you're at exercise first thing tomorrow morning," Greg shouted.

Confidence and courage are infectious, but so is cowardice. Both are able to spread through a group of men to bolster their ranks, or to ruin them. With this group of gutless men, their hidden cowardice was as crippling as a cancer, and it crept through the whole body of bullies, weakening them to the point of breaching their criminal code of conduct. They stuck Greg in, informing the screws that he was coming for them, and he was caught with a "dagger" prior to exercise.

I was taken out to exercise in the digger. The exercise yards were a sight to behold, as if the prison authorities reserved them as a special place for psychological impact. Dunedin was a step up from A-section, but was nicknamed "Beirut" by the screws themselves. It had three high fences topped with coil after coil of razor wire, which encircled the three solitary exercise pens. The wire looked as though it had been ripped out of the Somme itself and preserved – no longer threatening soldiers but growling at any juvenile delinquent who might consider climbing over the cages. I was taken to one of these pens for exercise. The Dunedin cells looked directly onto the pens, enabling the YOs to chat to each other through cages and bars which led to solitary cell windows. The cages outside the cells were covered with years of slimy spit. The freshest saliva clung to the layers of previous spit and formed cascading layers of frozen and solidified goo, a crude monument to the progress that Polmont was making in dealing with young men.

"Greg, is that you bro?" I said, peering through the caked cage of a solitary cell.

"Tony?" came the reply from within.

"Aye, bro, it's me. Come to the window."

Greg made his way to the window, slowly and painfully.

"What's wrong, mate?" I asked

"They done me, mate, big time," he replied.

"Who?" I said. "Who done you?"

"The screws, bro. They're off the scale in here."

Greg had been dragged down to Dunedin Unit and placed back in solitary after the gang of Glasgow lads had told the screws that he was going to attack them at exercise. While in the digger, he had had a dispute with the Nevis screws who had carted him down there and, true to their character and in keeping with their craving for brutality, they told him he was to be strip-searched. While Greg was putting his trousers back on, one notorious screw nicknamed "The Bull" had taken the opportunity to throw a hook. As Greg fell to the ground, they put the boot in. It was Greg's birthday.

"Mate, they can't keep doing this. We'll have to do something about it," I told him.

"I can't do anything," he said back.

Saddened to see my best friend so disheartened, I replied, "It's so good to see you, bro."

I missed my friend so much. He was closer to me than family. Ever since we were kids, we had done everything together, and seeing him like this affected me terribly.

"Happy birthday, mate," I said. We both laughed. Then I stretched out my hand through the bars and gobcage, in a feeble attempt to shake his hand. I managed to just touch his fingers and we both smiled.

"At least I got to see you today," I said.

After three days of cellular confinement, Greg and I were taken back to A-section. By now, the cowards had been integrated back into the mainstream of Nevis. In an entire wing that was 80 per cent Glaswegian, they now had numbers well and truly behind them. They had merged back into their sinister flock and were gaining confidence, like a murder of crows waiting for their next easy meal.

What they had not counted on was that Greg and I were not newborn lambs that would allow our eyes to be easily pecked out. In A-section we were out of association, but until our time in A-section was over, we would wait, and we would plan well.

They allowed us to have books in A-section at that time. My reading list was in keeping with the YO culture, wherein we all had our patron saints. These ranged from the South American drug baron Pablo Escobar to mad Frankie Fraser. Each YO dreamed of gaining the same notoriety. I had chosen as my special patron and idol Mark Chopper Reid, the Australian hit man and lunatic responsible for unprecedented prison violence in the 1970s within Australia's notorious Pentridge Prison. Throughout numerous prison wars, he came out alive. I kept his picture, ripped out from a book, on my wall to remind me that it was possible for one man to take on a prison.

Around that time, another Edinburgh lad was brought to A-section – Coco. He was brought in for badly scalding one of the Glaswegian camp with boiling water and melted sugar. He was a welcome addition to our two-man team. Before our arrival, Coco had long established himself fighting west coast guys, and at one point he had had to be placed on semi-protection. But when Greg arrived, he sent a message for Coco to get himself out immediately and stop shaming himself. So here we were, an unholy trinity, ready to take on an entire wing. There were a couple of other Edinburgh boys in the mainstream of Nevis Hall and we quickly made plans to get them signed up. Wee Bruno from Leith was sent a "stiffy" (an in-house letter passed through a neutral person to another gang) "enlisting his service", and one was also sent to Heegie, who was a good friend of ours from Broomhouse in Edinburgh. He would not need to be reminded of his duty to stand with us.

As the time approached for Greg and me to be let out of A-section and into the mainstream, you could have cut the atmosphere in Nevis Hall with a knife. Throughout the night I could hear the faint scratching of daggers being sharpened against brickwork as the wing was preparing for war.

***

Although on a heightened state of alert for the external struggle that lay ahead, still the demons nested within the blackness of my heart, continually clawing my mind into the shadows of my past.

How could I have done that?

Why was I this way?

There was a constant dread within the very pit of my stomach. These lurking memories were a nest of vipers striking and sinking their fangs deep into my conscience, injecting me with their poisonous condemnation and their toxic accusations. I wanted to howl with remorse. I felt forever on the brink of insanity – but there was no release.

***

The day finally came for us to leave A-section and join the mainstream. As we were placed into the new section, Greg and I had already planned an ambush. We had organized for it to kick off at recreation that evening, since there was no way it would be going ahead on their terms. They outnumbered us drastically. We would have to sniper them at a time when they least expected it.

Heegie, Greg, Coco, Bruno, and I went out to the exercise yard that morning. We stood with our backs to the wall while they all lined up at the other side, our five to their forty-odd. There were a few guys from other Scottish areas interspersed, walking with their heads firmly down, eyes fixed on their feet like their shoelaces were in need of urgent attention, desperately trying to ignore the elephant in the room. The Glasgow boys oozed confidence, their pride swelling as their numbers increased. We faced each other down across the exercise yard in anticipation. We formed a small circle. I asked Greg who he wanted to go for. It had to be now. If we left it until tonight, they could collect their weapons and we would be dead.

Greg said, "Let me get that guy with the big head."

"That's it, back in," shouted one of the screws, motioning for us to leave the yard and go back into the hall. Now was our chance. As we all moved back toward the door, we bottlenecked. Then Coco, Bruno, Heegie, Greg, and I weaved in and out of them, dropping them as we went. They were stunned that we had just attacked the lot of them. Greg and I were like boys back in the gym again, but this time it was west coast punchbags that we were hitting. They were so tightly packed as we merged going back on to the wing that it was hard for them to see who was who and what was happening, as we all wore the same bright red shirts in Nevis Hall. We used their numbers against them to strike confusion and panic as we picked off our targets. It wasn't long before we were scrapping with all of them.

As the screws hit the panic alarm we continued to throw punches, desperate to strike a decisive blow before the tidal wave of screws came in to disperse the emerging riot. I buzzed with adrenaline and excitement. A few months earlier, before I was remanded, I was meant to box for Scotland in Italy. Years of training were now unleashed. This wasn't an exhibition bout or even a title fight, yet I fought like I was fighting for my life. We needed to send a message to the entire prison that we would be up for it. Any time. Any place. Anyone.

Our small Edinburgh gang was dragged straight down to Dunedin's solitary cells. Each of us was slapped on a Rule 80, which meant we were to remain in solitary for a minimum of one month, while the Glasgow boys remained in Nevis with their black eyes and bruised egos. This wasn't just an in-house scrap: by striking a blow at the heart of Glasgow's up and coming gangsters, we had challenged the long-standing Glaswegian dominance of the Young Offenders Institution.

After the audacity of this attack, the Scottish Prison Service stated clearly on our intelligence reports that Greg and I were presently too dangerous to be kept in the same prison together.

5

Among the Tombs

HMYOI Polmont

"Tony, they're moving me out. I'm getting shipped up to Shotts' NIC." Because he had just turned twenty-one, Greg was graduating with full honours. While I was glad that he was getting out of this hellhole, I was sad to see him go. Coco and Heegie were also informed that they were being moved back to Saughton. They too were over twenty-one and were long overdue their trip to the cons. At only seventeen, I still had years left in this pit.

And so I remained among the tombs of solitary, cast into a living nightmare with accusing voices rising like wraiths, drawing me back again and again to feast on the horrors of my past. The torment was unbearable. It was as if inner demons rose up from within and took their place in the solitary cell with me. Shame, Despair, and Suicide, like some diabolical triumvirate, appeared. Shame was always the first to make a case and, with the subtlety of an ancient serpent, he spoke with a whisper: "I know your secrets that would scatter your friends and make your family shrink back with horror. Do you doubt me?"

With a gentle hush, a multitude of images were brought forth as he presented his case. I held my head in my hands, wishing desperately for it to stop, but no end came. I dug my nails into my face, my soul writhing as shame pinned me down and force-fed me the horrors of my rage, my lust, my greed, and my betrayals.

Despair interrupted: "No way back. No way forward. No way out."

Suicide came last, snaking forward with his hangman's noose clasped by pale hands with pale wrists, his voice sweet and sickly as honey: "Let me welcome you into my arms. I am able to make all pain cease."

***

After the month was over, the screws put me back into A-section, where I faced the hall again, but this time alone. Back to A-section; back to throwing bodily waste out of the window; back to planning how to stay alive. There would be no opportunity like the last. I would have to attack, on sight, the first Glaswegian I saw. As my cell opened, allowing me to get dinner from the cupboard from where it was served at the end of the section, I saw my chance. I nosedived straight over the hotplate, bringing my dagger down into the face of the Glaswegian serving food. Once more, I was carted heavily back to solitary. Once more, the demons had my full attention.

Back in Dunedin, the screws were as brutal as ever. I was tired of their aggression and continual disrespect. I hated them for their bullying and provocations. I hated them. From day one in Polmont, these screws had been on my case. Moreover, I hated them for beating up Greg. Finally I had had enough of them. As they opened up the cell to let me fill my water bottle, I ran forward and smashed an officer called Frank with a straight right hand across the jaw.

"Do you think we're animals down here?" I yelled.

He fell to the floor as the two other officers tried to pounce on me. I was filled with so much rage that they were thrown about as easily as empty tracksuits – until one of them crawled forward and grabbed my ankles. I hated it when people did this. As I bent down and began to squeeze and gouge his face, a sea of white shirts broke upon me. Punch after punch; kick after kick; a whole host of screws set about me.

"GET FRANK TO THE SURGERY NOW! GET HIM OUT OF HERE!"

I could hear the voices of supervising officers giving orders, even as they themselves were putting the boot in. "We're going to do you properly this time," they whispered in my ear.

They carted me off toward the "silent cell" within the segregation unit. The silent cell was soundproofed and contained padding on the doors. There were no beds and no furniture, only bare walls with spy holes placed in strategic locations for the screws or medics to keep an eye on you. It was a place for the most volatile prisoners to be held until they were deemed settled enough to return to the regular solitary cells. I was used to this, and by now I was fed up and weary of all this fighting. I hated who I had become; I hated my violent nature; most of all, I hated the fact that no matter how hard I tried, I could not escape my own prison of hatred and violence.

I passionately hated many people, but I reserved my deepest hatred for myself.

It was only a short distance to the silent cell, as it was contained within Dunedin Unit, but they drew out this thirty-five metre journey for as long as possible – dragging me to my feet then slamming me down on the ground, dragging me a few metres forward then slamming me back down. The beating on this journey became so intense that I wished desperately to pass out. Everything inside me wanted to scream, but I refused to allow myself to do so. Determined not to show any weakness, I allowed myself only to release guttural groans, as I knew other YOs were listening – some of them my enemies. Then, as they once again slammed me down to the floor, one officer took my wrist, stretched it out on the ground, bent it back, and then, lifting it high into the air, he cracked it off the concrete floor. Everything within me wanted to scream out as I felt my wrist crunch. Then, with the bone protruding from my wrist, they crushed it down, rolling it back and forth over the concrete. Searing waves of heat-filled pain coursed through my body, making me tremble. Still I didn't scream.

As I lay face down on the cold concrete floor, they lifted my wrist high into the air again, then repeatedly slammed it to the ground. I screamed. Their sick, determined mission to make all prisoners know what happens when a screw is attacked was finally fulfilled. The pain from their kicks and punches was immediately eclipsed by this new agony. The thought of going through this prolonged torment for even one second longer was insupportable. I started to involuntarily shake and convulse, as if my body was trying to shake off pain itself.

"Stop moving!" they shouted, and began stamping on my legs and every other part of my quaking body. My inability to stop shaking only incited further hatred. The pain was driving me mad. Forward. Two steps. BANG off the ground. Forward. Two steps. BANG off the ground. Then back to rolling my wrecked wrist over the concrete. They lifted me up and moved me forward just a few metres, but no more than that – they were determined to savour every second of this cycle of torture.

"Leave him alone!" yelled a voice.

The YOs started banging on their doors, even the Glasgow boys. They all shouted as I was dragged past their cells, and they lay down and spoke words of encouragement through the gaps under the steel doors,

"On you go, Tony boy."

"You can do it."

"In your stride, Tony. In your stride."

They kicked their doors constantly in a futile effort to get the screws to stop. The steel hatches on the doors of the solitary cells slammed open and shut, as the YOs and screws hurled obscenities at one another. Never before had I longed so much to reach the silent cell, but when it came there was no respite. I could hear the muffled echoes of boot after boot piling into the cell after they carted me through the doors. They stripped me naked and forced me to stand against the back wall of the cell. An army of white shirts and hate-filled eyes stared at me. Even with such numbers bearing down on me, they still treated me like I was a time bomb, ready to explode. While they remained extremely cautious, I, in reality, was finished.

A short, round nurse, her yellowed face bearing witness to a lifetime's nicotine habit, came forward to examine me, as was the standard routine after a prisoner had been restrained.

"Right, it's time to stop being the hard man now," came her piercing, pitiless screech.

Nurses were just screws in different uniforms. There was no professional impartiality. She hated me as much as they did. As she examined my broken body, she continued to spout sarcastic comments. "Did you think you could get away with it?" she scoffed. "Next time you'll know better."

Helplessly pinned against the wall, I managed to muster the only form of resistance I had left. Lifting up my head, I spat in her face. The rest became a blur of pain as the horde of screws set upon me again.

As they left, I lay on the ground – a curled-up ball of misery. Nevertheless, I knew that as soon as the padded steel doors of the silent cell shut, they would be staring at me through spy hatches in the walls designed for observation. I had never, in seven years of boxing, been put on the canvas, and here I was lying on the floor. Determined to have the last word, I dragged myself up, clasping my mangled wrist to my side, and began shadow-boxing with my one remaining good hand, knowing that this would leave a lasting psychological impact on those watching.

After several hours, there came a shout. I was by now sitting on the floor. "Hands against the back wall."

Locks turned, the door opened, and the supervising officer came into the cell, followed by a large group of officers.

"Tony, if we place you back in your cell, are my officers going to be safe?" he asked.

"No," I replied, resolutely refusing to give any ground.

"Not good enough," said the SO, and they turned and walked out of the cell.

After this scenario had repeated itself several times, and after several subsequent hours of standing in a concrete cell naked, I was freezing when they finally put me back into a regular solitary cell and sent for the doctor to look at my injuries. The doctor came in to see me, took one look at my wrist, and barked, "X-ray", while throwing a disgusted look at the screws. As they closed the door, I could hear the screws pleading with him on the other side. "Does he really need to go for an X-ray?"

"Yes," the doctor insisted firmly.

Right after this, they took me out to the hospital and I was given a temporary wrist brace, as the swelling was too bad for any other treatment at that time. Within the wrist brace there were two pieces of aluminium. I took out one of these seven-inch pieces of metal, and when I returned to the cell I began to sharpen it on the stone floor, fully intending to use it on the officer who had done this to me.

When I got back from the hospital, the place stank. It turned out that while I was at the hospital, the other YOs had initiated a dirty protest in solidarity. The whole unit stood alongside one another, even my enemies, appalled at the treatment I had received. The smell of excrement within the unit was horrendous – every cell reeked with putrid protestation. The screws grumbled bitterly at having to work in these nauseating conditions. Every day, the smell worsened as prisoners began to throw even their urine out under the doors to the corridors on which the screws patrolled. They were totally disgusted, and came into our cells only to deliver our meals, and even then wearing forensic suits. When I returned to my cell,

I smeared excrement on the wall, writing in large, foot-high letters, "Oppression breeds aggression."

We put excrement around our wrists and on our bodies to stop the screws from coming near us. Some YOs ripped up their bedsheets and made bandannas; they smeared their faces with faeces like it was warpaint, and called themselves Rambo, Tarzan, GI Jobby, and so on. One YO was "unfortunately" unable to identify with us in this protest, owing to a lack of the necessary bodily productions. He therefore began calling on us, asking for a "square-up." Essentially, this meant smuggling some excrement to him, with some thread and a weight slid under the door. Such was the desperation to protest against the brutality, that one lad was willing to use the waste of another to express exteriorly the prison's subhuman conditions.

This protest continued for several days. But the atmosphere in Dunedin, like the smell it created, grew worse. As the tension between prisoners and screws grew more and more hostile, their brutality grew in proportion.

A couple of days after this protest had ended, I heard the familiar rattle of the meal trolley coming down the corridor and stopping at my door. As I stepped forward to receive my food, I glanced down the corridor and spotted Ken mopping the floor. Ken was a protection prisoner who was serving time for rape. Protection prisoners were the only prisoners allowed into the Dunedin Unit because young offenders like us would not discuss anything or communicate with them, as they were wholly despised. They were considered "safe" to carry out the task of cleaning the solitary wing, because no one could get to them. Ken was the same guy who, along with Iain

Osbourne, had beaten me as a kid and smashed a brick over my head. I went back into my cell and busted my aluminium dagger out of the spine of the book in which I had concealed it in preparation for a certain screw. When the meal trolley returned to collect the plates, I kicked it out of the way. Gripping my dagger, I bolted down the corridor as the screws shouted, "NO, TONY! DON'T!"

Ken heard the shouts of the officers and started to run, but I caught up. I missed his throat and got him in the shoulder several times as he tried to get away. The screws were terrified. They didn't even attempt to restrain me. They just let me walk back into my cell. Later in the day when they came back to give me my dinner, the screws shook so much as they handed me my plate that the food was spilling everywhere. "Look what you're doing to us," one of them said.

It was clear that the greatest strain for them was my unpredictability and my liability to react at the slightest perceived insult. The atmosphere between the screws and me became so intense that I would not speak to them or ask them for anything.

Three officers came for me and took me into the office in the solitary unit. One officer, Tom, asked me to sit down. He said, "Tony, a few years ago my son died. I can't stay at home because I think about him too much. I have to come in to work to take my mind off things. Now, because of you, the stress of coming in to work is too much."

He took a well-worn picture from his wallet of a boy of around twelve and put it on the table in front of me. I don't quite know why he did this, but at that moment I was totally stunned and unable to find the words to say anything. I hated who I was and who I had become. I could see my reflection in the steel panel behind Tom, and I no longer recognized myself. I was wholly consumed with hate, no longer in control.

The screws were always on edge now. They handcuffed me to two officers wherever I went, and I would be chained to one on my left and another on my right. Seeing this, YOs across the jail would bang their doors and shout, "TONY'S GONNAE GET YI! TONY'S GONNAE GET YI!" If I was taken out to exercise, they would ensure no other prisoner was adjacent to the solitary yard I was in, despite there being no way of seeing, let alone getting near, another prisoner. My phone calls were closely monitored all the time, and my mail was screened. I had to take my visits with screws standing around me, staring at me and my visitors. This only served to fuel my hatred of them. Still, I hated myself more than anyone. I was steeped in hostility, as if plunged into an ocean of contempt. In this habitat, it wasn't just the screws who recognized this. By now everyone seemed wary of me. Wherever I went, I seemed to cast a shadow.

***

As soon as I was allowed back on to the wing, I started strategizing. It became second nature to count how many pool cues there were at recreation, where they were stored, how many guys were in each camp, who would need to be taken out first. Where could I stash weapons, what kind of characters the screws were, their mindsets, their shift patterns? I was a restless wreck eaten away by distrust. I followed my own personal policy of always being the first to act, never hesitating or speculating. After any argument or disagreement, I would act first. This was extreme, but in Polmont small matters became big matters – in no time. Problems, even imagined problems, would be magnified. Take an unacknowledged greeting, for example. One prisoner walks past another and says, "Alright?" But the other doesn't respond. This can send the YO who was ignored into a state of all-consuming paranoia. *Is he trying to wind me up? Does he think he's better than me? Is he going to try something on me?*

The mind, with too much time on its hands, begins to exhaust every possible avenue, but always with the twistedness that comes from a heart conditioned by violence. Not long after this the razor is melted onto the toothbrush. In reality, the person may not have heard the greeting. Maybe he had just put the phone down on the girlfriend who'd been cheating on him, or received some other bad news which had folded him in on himself. In reality he was oblivious to everyone and everything, not just someone saying "Alright?" Then more suffering is added through the wound he receives from an old friend, out of nowhere. The scar will remain with him as a reminder, for the rest of his life.

My own chronic paranoia pervaded everything. It manifested itself in listening to conversations between prisoners through pipe holes along the floor of a cell, or lying awake at night trying to pick out the treacherous whispers from the conniving councils that were held in the wee hours of the morning. I would listen to who other YOs were going to attack, when, and how they would do it, always looking out for the faint hint of anything that could be interpreted as a threat to me. Always watching, always waiting, always ready. No peace!

Throughout my time in Polmont, my family came to see me regularly, especially my parents. From one visit to the next, I watched them age. The constant anxiety I was putting them under was severe. They would hear on the street about some of the things taking place in Polmont, and almost every time they heard from me I was in the digger. I hated what I was doing to them, and I hated the animal they had to visit.

"I will stop the violence. I will get my head down and get out."

But what I willed I could not do. Instead, I gave them nothing but broken promises. I just could not control myself – as soon as someone even looked at me the wrong way, I would attack. I had become so violent and unpredictable that I seriously feared myself. Yet, despite all of my broken promises, the love of my family was always ready to hope, always prepared to believe, always able to trust. It never gave up. This caused me anguish that was deeper than any physical pain. Though for their sake I desperately strived for change, I could not do it, no matter how hard I tried. My family meant everything to me, but my self-hatred and the cheapness with which I regarded my own life and that of others proved devastating.

After taking a blade down another guy's face because of an insult, I was dragged back to the digger. This time HMYOI had had enough, and the governor wrote a letter to the Scottish Government asking to have me reclassified as an adult. At the age of nineteen, I was kicked out of the most violent prison in Scotland. After two years in this pit, thirteen months of which were in solitary, I was moving on.

6

In the Land of Deep Darkness a Light Has Dawned

HMP Edinburgh (Saughton)

My stomach turned as the smell hit me. It was the smell
of Saughton, aka HMP Edinburgh. Every prison has its
own scent, brought about by its own particular mixture
of cheap disinfectants, but for me, the smell of Saughton
is the smell of despair. The aroma entered my nostrils.
In a split second it transcended the senses and, having
captured the essence of that darkest period of my life
two years earlier, it now demanded my full attention. It
forced me to recall the anxiety, insomnia, and emotional
desolation of those first few weeks in solitary at the start
of my sentence. It is strange, the way a scent is able to
arrest a moment, taking it captive and enabling it to be
revisited whenever it is experienced.

Now that the Government had given the Scottish

Prison Service permission to have me reclassified and moved to the cons – basically I was booted out of the YOs for being too volatile – I returned to Saughton not through the reception, dog boxes, and usual route, but through the side of the jail in the back of a van. This was the route reserved for "difficult" prisoners. As the van snaked its way through the prison buildings, the fences stretched high into the heavens, proudly challenging the sky, and smothering our dreams and aspirations. The razor wire crowning these fences grinned menacingly as I was driven through, their ragged rows of sharp teeth welcoming me into the belly of the beast.

Through the van's blackened windows I could see prisoners from various wings out in the yards. It was a summer's day and most of the guys were lying down sunbathing. When they saw the van, they jumped up and came to the fence, curious to see who was inside. The van slowed at the segregation unit, and cons from all over the prison pressed their faces further into the fences to get a better look. I realized that some of the men looking back at me were prisoners I had known in the YOs institution. These men had once been strong, fit lads, but now they glared at the van with gaunt faces and dark sunken eyes, like dim lights flickering in deep caves. Their skinny bodies now betrayed them, announcing that they had turned to heroin to get through their sentences.

A screech of the brakes was followed by the sound of doors slamming. The back of the van opened and I stepped out into the bright daylight. Voices began murmuring, "Its Tony boy... Aye... Tony Gielty."

Then came the shouts and cheers of, "ON YA GO, TONY BOY... RUNNING AMOK IN THE YOs... ON YA GO!"

The scene was akin to a new animal being brought into a zoo, with the spectators lining up to watch it enter its new habitat. I knew for certain, then and there, that any hopes of keeping my head down and leaving behind an unwanted reputation had vanished.

Here I was, back where it had all started. The smell was the same and so were the screws – even their clothing was the same. In contrast to the usual uniform of shiny boots, black trousers, and pristine white shirts dignified with safety ties, this mob wore clothing made up of loose, commando-style trousers and polo-necked shirts, well suited for dealing with the segregated prisoners – the violent ones.

"Hey, Tony, how'd you get on in Polmont?" one screw asked when showing me to my cell.

"Easy time," I lied, determined never to show any weakness. The system was always watching, waiting to see where your weaknesses lay. I had been weak before, telling the screws in Polmont that I really wanted to see my disabled brother and how he couldn't make visits because of his disability. They noted this, gave me one compassionate visit, then promptly turned it into a carrot and stick. I hated them all. Screws and cons alike studied one another for where to apply pressure, when to do it, and how it should be done. In our world, cons could always say, "At least we're not screws," and screws could always say, "At least we're not cons." In truth, we loved to hate each other. Solzhenitsyn was right: "Men must see themselves not as the worst of men."

As he handed me my towel and bedding, the screw standing at my cell door commented, "You must have caused some bother to end up back here so early."

Another butted in, "Shotts didn't want to take you

because you're so young. We don't know why you're here either."

Behind their friendliness I could clearly see their fear of having me in their unit.

"Phone your governor; he'll tell you why," I said, casually walking into my cell, trying to show by my actions that I had some control.

As I lay down on the bed and turned away, they understood I was finished talking. They gently closed the cell door and I, looking for something to keep my mind off things, started reading the names of prisoners and statements that had been scratched into the stainless steel furniture by previous cons:

"Heegie was here, doing time feeling fine, yeeha 2003!!!"

"Jamie H – here we go again!!!"

"EYT on top, non stop!!!"

"It's the bold Ball-kicking, Lockback-flicking, Jaw-Ripping, Techno-jigging, Buckfast-swigging, Ecto-popping, Coke-snorting, Dope-toking, Screw-bashing, Giro-cashing – John McCleod."

"Dave P – hated but rated!!!"

"Jimmy E is a beast."

"Banksy is a Grass! Pure wrong one..."

***

"Hi, Tony, how are you?" The dog squad was back. (Other prisoners and I called this group the dog squad on account of their malice.)

"What is it?" I asked, looking them up and down, mistrustful of this new tone.

"It won't be long now before you get back up the wing and out of here."

This was so awkward. Once they had treated me terribly, but now they showed respect. I wanted them to be harsh so I could hate. That would be easier; it would be far simpler that way. Otherwise I might start to soften toward them.

I recalled a not-so-serious example of the dog squad's malice. It was back before I left to go to Polmont and they had humiliated me by sending me into the most violent prison in Scotland without giving me a haircut. It is really important among YOs to have tidy hair, not only for their own reputation, but also in order to be presentable to families: we would do all we could to stop them worrying. Shaggy hair and beards often implied a person had given up. For any YO, not having a haircut is bad enough, but with me, it's worse. My thick hair doesn't just grow long; it also grows fat. Instead of growing downward, it grows up and out like a ginger afro. I was sent to Polmont looking ridiculous!

In sharp contrast to the YOs, cons are very relaxed. There is far more solidarity between them, as cons are less concerned with building up their damaged egos. On the flip side, however, cons are dominated by one of two things: drugs or money, but mostly drugs.

During this period I sensed I was witnessing the last phases of a major prison transition. It was the transition from the old-style Victorian prisons to the modern, block-built buildings, and with this change in architecture came a change in culture. Prisons, especially adult prisons, were and are still becoming more like hospitals – or, to put it bluntly, psychiatric wards. This is particularly reflected in the mornings when prisoners line up for their medication. Methadone seemed to be the only solution on offer for "stabilizing" drug users. Hundreds of them would queue to receive their daily dose of green fluid. They stretched so far along the corridors that we called it the "Green Mile". No prisoner on methadone could function for long without his dose – it well deserved its title "the Liquid Handcuff".

In anticipation of this culture, I had smuggled some heroin in with me for currency, through the gardeners' work party in Polmont. This heroin would allow me to get hold of "essentials". Not long after I was let out of the Seg Unit, a lockback knife was sneaked from one wing to another until, through my friend L. Roy, it reached me.

I was placed on Ingleston top flat with all the other long-term cons and quickly began to find out how it all worked. It was simple: whoever controlled the smack controlled the jail.

I set about finding out different means of smuggling it in. Conversations had to be conducted carefully: prison is full of grasses – particularly on a long-term wing, as the rewards are considerable. For these grasses, any information provided may speed their progression to an open estate prison, where they can receive weekend leave every month. And it also makes the time inside their current jail considerably easier, as they will be offered the best jobs, like hall pass-man (cleaner), hotplate (serving the food), or kit-pass (doing the washing). People on these duties are allowed out of their cells way more and are given much more freedom within the prison system.

So I set about discussing the matter of smuggling with a few people I knew I could trust. I quickly set up a system, working with a lifer who was on the TFF (Training for Freedom) programme. He was among the low-risk cons several blocks below us, and allowed to go out to the community for work experience. For him, this was a kind of intermediate stage prior to being moved to an open estate prison – the final step before release after having spent more than twelve years inside. Although on the verge of freedom, he was willing to risk it all for the opportunity to make money and take drugs.

This guy's situation was the perfect way for me to get stuff in. My contact would meet him on the street with the gear and then he would bring it in with him. Incidentally, this particular prisoner was especially suited for the job as he was exceptionally overweight and able to conceal large amounts of drugs under the rolls of fat on his body. He always brought in one ounce of heroin and four ounces of cannabis. The four ounces of cannabis I smoked with my cellmate and other friends; the heroin would be sold. There are just over 28 grams in an ounce of heroin. I would divide this into eighths (3.5 grams) which I sold to eight "reliable" cons for £250 each, and I collected a total of £2,000 per week. An ounce of heroin is a significant amount in prison as, when it is broken down and sold on by other cons, it can have a net value of £7,000. Prisoners will take a regular ballpoint pen and unscrew the tip (the little black part at the end of the pen, not the lid). This is then filled with approximately 0.2 g of heroin, and is known as a "Nifty"; the name derived from its price, which is fifty pounds.

The money for these sales was handled on the outside through postal orders or a network of friends and family who received instructions from the men inside. A prisoner would tell a friend or family member on the outside where to take the money to. This would be done via a mobile phone or subtly on a visit. When the money reached my requested destination on the outside, they would receive their drugs on the inside. Others in prison would operate out of trust and provide the drugs prior to any arrival of money, relying solely on their reputation to ensure money would be paid. This often resulted in violence when the recipient couldn't pay.

I quickly began to establish myself in Saughton through my dealing. It cost me £1,000 for an ounce of heroin: that gave £1,000 clear profit each week. My plan was simple: stay out of trouble and make plenty of money for my release. I still had years ahead of me, so this was a good opportunity to save.

The contacts I was able to make among the cons were far better than the YOs, as I was sharing a wing with career criminals from all over the world. One such contact was Moe, a fellow con with whom I had become friends. His family were from Afghanistan and he often told me about his uncle, to whom he wanted to introduce me. Moe kept asking if I would go into "business" with them: his uncle owned poppy fields back home and needed more European partners. However, I also discovered that his uncle was unwilling to go directly into business with Moe himself because, as Moe so succinctly put it, "If it all goes wrong he cannot be doing the killing of me – his nephew."

Some opportunities were more appealing than others! But this represented the reality that prison is such a place of opportunity for the career criminal, and valuable and powerful contacts are easily made in preparation for life on the outside. I started to have Valium smuggled in too as, although I was in a more stable environment, my inner world was still completely chaotic and full of pain. The hash helped, but sometimes made me worse; Valium was a means to block it out. However, with Valium, things just got far worse. I should have known better: I had watched scores of young men come into prison as a result of excessive use of Valium, which had caused them to act in a completely crazy way. They would tell me how they had woken up in a police cell to be informed that they had just killed their best friend.

Ignoring all the cautionary stories, I began to take serious amounts of Valium – sometimes more than fifty pills in a weekend. This would cause me to forget what I was doing to people. At times I would have flashbacks of walking into the cells of other prisoners in the morning while they were just waking up and putting blades to their throats threatening to kill them for this or that, or of almost killing my cellmate after I had taken too many pills. I would lose count of the number of pills I had and then think, *He must have taken some.* In reality, I couldn't even remember how many I'd swallowed.

I was losing it completely. Before, I had understood what I was doing and how I was feeling; now I was running on autopilot and heading for a major crash. The prison officers became so wary of me that when they came to my cell in the middle of the day and found me smoking a joint, they would just ask me to spray something to take the smell away. At the age of nineteen, as everyone distanced themselves from me, I had the screws in my hand. I thought I had complete control in this new environment but, as ever, I was not in control of myself.

Yet, there was always someone ready to challenge. As I walked past a prisoner that everyone considered to be a psycho, as he cared nothing for either his reputation or his release – a dangerous man with nothing to lose – he grunted and snarled, "What are you growling at?"

I flew at him but my punch missed him – probably because of the Valium. We began rolling around the floor, trying to bite and gouge bits off each other, and it wasn't long before we were both dragged down to the Seg Unit to see the governor.

After we had both been disciplined, we were put back on the landing. When I got back on the wing, I shouted to the pass-man, a guy called Frankie, to come over to my cell. Just before coming into jail Frankie had lost his eye after my mate Matt tried to blow his head off with a shotgun. Matt had called him to the window of his flat from the street in the Granton area of Edinburgh. When Frankie looked out, Matt fired his shotgun, and Frankie lost the eye through the lead spread.

Lifting my cell's spy hatch, Frankie said, "Alright, mate?"

"Go round there and tell that idiot we're settling this tonight!" I ordered him.

"Okay, Tony," he replied.

In no time Frankie was back, as white as a ghost. "He's tooled to the teeth," he informed me, gesturing with his hands to indicate the considerable size of the psycho's blade. "He said, 'He's easy.'"

"Good," I replied firmly. "I'll do that head case tonight."

When the time came, a con came over and pointed to a cell some fifty feet along the wing. The door was open. "He's in that one."

I put my hand in my pocket, grabbed my sturdy lockback, and opened it inside my pocket, away from the cameras – it would be too late to open it in the cell. As I approached the cell I began to play out in my mind how this would go down. *Big lunges with downward swipes for certain*, I thought. He was way taller than me.

Just as I got to the cell, a con grabbed me. "Tony, he

doesn't want to go ahead," he said, gesturing for me to come away from the cell.

"Eh?" I replied, confused.

"He doesn't want to, man," the con insisted again.

It turned out that even this psycho didn't want to challenge me. He had pleaded with this con to come and speak to me, to stop it at the last minute. There was no one willing to stand in my way: not the screws, not even the toughest or maddest of the cons.

***

I became more unstable. This was not helped by the Valium. I would fly off the handle at the least thing and behave in the most unpredictable ways. I would walk up to the pantry at mealtimes in front of the screws and cons and bang the stainless steel serving area, laughing at people and making fun of them openly. At other times I would ridicule them just to get a reaction. No one stopped me. Then, after I suspected a guy from Dundee of "getting wide", I knocked him across the cell and started to crack him so badly that blood smeared all over the floor and walls. Some cons eventually pulled me off him and got him out. The screws left me alone, but then they came through my cell door in the wee hours of the morning, dragging me back to the digger. Again.

***

"People everywhere will be horrified to hear of such barbarous acts committed in their midst," said Judge Lord Bracadale before sentencing Hatchy, who was described by the BBC at the time of his sentence as

"Scotland's most vicious killer". He was serving life for two murders, murders that had shocked the country when it had emerged during his trial how he had tortured his victims over drug debts before killing them. His story caused further horror when it was revealed that he had dismembered and burned the body of his own cousin by calmly lighting a fire in his back garden and drinking beer while systematically burning his arms and legs. This was after playing football with the severed head, then placing it on his mantelpiece for several days to serve as an example to others.

"It's a pleasure to be in the same digger with you, Tony boy," came a voice from over the wall. The Glaswegian accent was coming from the solitary exercise yard next to mine.

"Aye, how are you doing, Hatchy?" I asked.

Hatchy had been sent to the Edinburgh Seg Unit after my best mate Greg had attacked a screw in Glenochil. Hatchy and Greg were banged up in separate Seg Units, despite the fact that Hatchy hadn't done anything. However, the prison officers recognized that he and Greg had established such a strong friendship that to take one of them out of mainstream without removing the other meant the screws were still liable to be subject to retaliation. Consequently, they were separated and isolated.

Hatchy arrived alongside me in the digger at a time when I had become very concerned about the way I was living and, in particular, the way I was going to end up. The prison authorities had exhausted every avenue with me in their endeavours to get me to change. I now saw with chilling certainty that my options had run out. It looked for sure as though there was no other road for me than that which the prisoners called the "Ghost Train".

Even Hatchy, described by the media as Scotland's worst killer, had told me, "Tony, you need to go see the priest."

The Ghost Train was no place for any soul, especially not one as young as nineteen. It consists of continuous solitary confinement for years on end. A prisoner is taken from prison to prison and held in each establishment's Seg Unit for three months before being moved to another solitary unit. This is done to ensure that the offender has very little time to settle into a routine, making it more difficult for them to plan any disorder or disruption. It is a "last resort" to ensure the safety of both prisoners and screws.

By now I had been in jail for approximately two and a half years and had witnessed the chilling aftermath in the lives of others who had undergone the Ghost Train. Some guys remained on it for periods of up to four or five years. They had often been responsible for rioting, hostage taking, drug smuggling, and other extreme actions. Prisoners recognized as having too much power and influence would also be put on the Ghost Train, as such influence may not just be exercised over other inmates, but can also extend to screws and other officials. Whether by money or threats – like bribes or finding out a family member's address – this influence can become a cancer within the prison, eating away the control and authority of the governing forces. Thus, the governor must resort to placing the person on the Ghost Train.

Needless to say, those disembarking the GT after years of seclusion were not the men they once had been. They were the prisoner wandering the exercise yard alone, like a wounded animal desperately trying to keep up with the pack, their brokenness evident to all. Often unable to rid themselves of the social and psychological damage that had contributed to their exclusion from others, they remained a haunting reminder of the impact of sustained solitary confinement. Many who had left the GT were unable to deal with the pressures of social interaction and would inwardly pine for the simplicity of being alone and not having to face others. This created very volatile and dangerous individuals. They would often attack another person, slashing or stabbing them without warning or cause, with the sole intention of securing a sustained period back in the familiarity of solitary.

One prisoner who entered the GT, named Stevie, had a solid criminal reputation. Described as a go-ahead, he had been highly respected on the outside; by the time he left the GT he was considered a freak. He suffered terribly from paranoia – always thinking that someone was out to get him, or that the screws were setting him up. While on the GT he had accumulated many neurotic traits. A less serious example of this was demonstrated whenever he was in the gym. He would go onto the punchbag but never hit it with any real force. When asked why he did this, he insisted that his reason for doing so was "'coz the screws put nuts and bolts inside the bag to break my hands".

At other times he would float around the punchbag displaying an utterly exhausted appearance. When asked what on earth he was doing, he would reply, "I always make it look as if I'm knackered, so if anyone tries to do me in, they'll think I'm finished. Then I will smash them." Stevie had been irreparably damaged through years of being in the digger.

***

I continued to hate myself more and more, and it seemed that every hour increased this. My real prison remained the interior life of my thoughts and emotions. It was as if a darkness had infected me and I was unable to enjoy the slightest relief from this inner pain. Though time in solitary often intensified this experience of inward desolation and served to magnify the pain, mainstream prison added just as much difficulty. I was often astonished to see prisoners who could smile and laugh and I would long for the ability to find release from my torment. I wanted to change so much, not just for my sake and sanity, but for my family who loved me.

While I was wrestling with all of these issues, the screws asked me to move to another cell. I refused. The cell they wanted me to go into was freezing and had a cracked window which let the cold air through. It hadn't changed from when I had first visited this digger two and half years ago – back then I had blocked my toilet deliberately so I would be moved out of it.

"You need to move," said one of the screws sheepishly.

"What?" I said, knocking the food he was trying to give me out of his hand.

The alarm was pressed and I attacked them. We wrestled and rolled about the floor, the sound of leather boots squeaking against and adding fresh scuff marks to the polished floors. This screeching mingled with the sound of keys hitting steel doors, creating the familiar theme tune that had been accompanying me for years. Meanwhile, as more officers came flowing through doors and walls like insects, I could hear "Scotland's worst killer" directing hate-filled and disturbing roars toward the screws: "Do you want to start? Do you? Come ahead then!"

It wasn't long before each screw had gone for one of my limbs and I was being dragged into the silent cell.

Some time later, the door opened and the same screws I had been fighting with stood in front of me. "Tony, is there anyone we can get to talk to you, anyone who can get through to you?" they asked.

They recognized my desperate situation. I was nineteen and heading for the GT. I believe it is likely they did not want to see someone so young being put through that and, out of an undeserved concern, they asked, "Is there anyone who can help?"

Undoubtedly they were thinking along the lines of a psychologist or psychiatrist, but just then, I remembered that Hatchy had suggested I "go see the priest". Usually I would have sworn at the screws and told them where to go, but on this occasion I didn't.

"I want to speak to the priest. Only he can help me." They were perplexed at this. I think they had hoped that I would wish to see a specialist. But they agreed and closed the door. Later they came back and escorted me to the exercise yard. The exercise yards in solitary resembled large kennels, sectioned by huge concrete walls with a grille on top and bars at the entrance. If anyone needed to speak with a segregated prisoner, they would have to come to the grille gate and speak through the bars.

When Father John MacFadden came to see me, there was something deeply disturbing about the man, something I couldn't work out. When he came to the grille, it was his stare that unsettled me most. He didn't look at me in the same way countless prisoners and prison officers would look at me. His stare was different. It wasn't the look of governors and wing managers when they glared at me on their weekly rounds. It was the opposite of the indifference that the nurses demonstrated. It really troubled me. For years I had been looked upon as an animal. Indeed, I believed I was an animal and was convinced that I could be nothing else. Yet there remained an approachable kindness in his eyes – eyes that were not telling me I was subhuman or heaping upon me the familiar judgment I was accustomed to and deserved. He stood there in such contrast to the three prison officers, who were more concerned for their safety and who saw only a crazy young man.

But the most shocking thing for me was when Fr John insisted that the officers allow him to enter the exercise yard with me. "I would like to speak *with* him," he said to the prison officers. To my amazement, they agreed.

Right there and then, I began to feel shame and deep regret for the life I had been living. When Fr John entered the yard and the screws closed the gate behind him, feelings of horror encircled me as I considered my own life in comparison to his.

With me? I thought. *Why does he want to see me? Why would he even care enough to speak to me?* I was bewildered. These "whys" caused a sharp and piercing pain to enter my heart which, in a moment, compelled me to consider the disaster which was my life.

When Fr John extended his hand to me, I was even more disturbed, and when he asked me how I was, I just found myself opening up to him and explaining, "Father, there's no helping somebody like me."

He calmly changed the subject completely and started to tell me about his life. "Do you know what I was before I was a priest?"

"Tell me," I mumbled.

"I was a bank manager. I had everything, Tony –

money, cars, women, the lot – everything that's supposed to make you happy; and I never was."

Then he told me that, while attending a work night out, he heard the Spice Girls' song "Wannabe", and the words unexpectedly forced him to question what he really wanted in life. His vocation as a priest was birthed out of this, but more than that: he began to experience the peace of knowing Jesus Christ. He realized that only in Him could true joy and peace be found.

My mind shrank away from this as I remembered my situation. I still had years ahead of me in prison, along with all the enemies and scores that were in need of being settled and, on top of all this, the Ghost Train was coming for me! *I've got all these problems and he's on about the Spice Girls!* I thought.

I demanded that the screws take me back inside. After that "weird" chat with Father John, I was keen to get back to the familiarity of my cell. It contained very little, except a flask of hot water which was refilled after meals and a small soapbox radio which the screws had given me to keep me quiet. So on my return, I made myself a cup of lukewarm jail tea, sat back on my bed, and turned the radio on.

I sat bolt upright in astonishment as the sound of that very song filled my cell.

7

The Voice of One Crying in the Wilderness

"Body of Christ," he whispered, gently placing the Eucharist in my hands and, in effect, reviving a goodness from the roots of my early life. Fr John, through his testimony and now through the Body of Christ, kindled that tiny flame of light that had been left unlit since childhood.

After hearing the very song he had described, I had asked to see him again, and now he had returned, carrying the Eucharist and the word of God.

After his second visit, I noticed that I could think of nothing but Jesus. Like a person falling in love, I was consumed with thoughts of God. I felt my heart soften ever so slightly, as if fresh water had been poured onto the hard, cracked earth of my heart. I had so much time on my hands now, yet through it all I found myself continually recalling the long-buried memories of God from my childhood. I remembered how much I had once loved

Jesus; how I had wandered the playground after hearing about the martyrs, sincerely inquiring of the other kids if they too would "die for Jesus"? I also recalled running to solitary places and climbing trees to be alone, and looking at pictures of the saints. Innocent and beautiful, these memories now returned in a sweet manner. They were like a thin shaft of light into the dark cave of my heart, and I welcomed them. Yet surely all these were just the pious memories of an unsullied period of innocence? Wasn't it just a section of my life that remained untouched; a rose garden which now, through recollection, could be nostalgically revisited within this dark place? Yet with every wandering step of my mind in this garden of God came light and longing. Unconsciously, I found my heart calling for Him again, a weak whisper trying to span a deep chasm.

I had now spent fifteen months of my sentence in solitary confinement. Thanks to what could only have been the prayers of Fr John, I wasn't placed on the Ghost Train but was instead moved to Glenochil, a maximum security prison situated not far from the historic town of Stirling at the feet of the Ochil Hills. This prison housed many of Scotland's killers and criminals, and I would be situated in the long-term wing, among those serving life and extensive sentences.

I was placed in a cell with Gary, a man who had heard about me through the grapevine and did all he could to make me welcome, even sharing his belongings with me and taking the time to roll me a smoke. As he placed the stringy tobacco in the wafer thin rolling paper, I could see that he was anxious. His big, powerful hands were shaking, and the sweat seeping through his pores caused the paper to stick to his fingers. I watched him closely before realizing I wasn't helping the situation. I turned away to unpack and take the pressure off him.

"You can choose your friends but not your cellmates," I said.

We both laughed.

"Wow, mate, I heard you were a psycho."

I began to express how I realized I needed to change before I killed someone or got killed, and how I just needed to leave this whole gang scene behind. Gary looked hugely relieved, and at once we began an open and honest friendship. Gary tried to help, offering advice from his own life experiences, yet I didn't know how to change. My idea of staying out of trouble was simply to do my best not to fight. So my plan was just to kick back, smoke some dope, and chill out till I got out.

Gary, my new "co-pilot" (cellmate), was quite different from the other co-pilots I'd had. Before his sentence he'd spent several years in the Foreign Legion, a truth evidenced by his regimented actions, scrupulous cleanliness, and annoying habit of singing in French.

"When you get to Marseilles, you surrender your passport," he said, lying back on the bed, staring upwards, as if his bunk were a hammock on some tropical island and not the prison cell we were sharing. He was relaxed now, having realized I wasn't some monster that would cut him up as soon as he slept. He made doing time look casual; he was like a man accustomed to far greater hardships. His face was worn and full of stress lines which indicated he had indeed seen tougher times. "After that they run some checks on you," he continued, "and when they're assured you'll be able to meet the physical and psychological demands of the *Légion Étrangère,* it's then you get a new identity!"

"A new identity?" I asked, trying to smother my intense interest.

"Aye, the training is brutal, but if you want to get away from it all, it's definitely one way to do it. I'd still be there if my Commanding Officer hadn't threatened to kill me, man." He stated this with a fearful face, and followed it with a flurry of angry French words. *"Comment oser que..."* A few moments passed. "But, if you can finish..." he sighed longingly, "you get a French passport and citizenship in many places across the world – the *Légion* will take care of you."

Instantly, I was hooked. *A new identity: that's it!* My mind raced and raced: this was it! *No matter how brutal the training... it's worth it. No matter how tough the officers, no matter what the cost... I want this second chance at life... to abandon my shame and bury my past... no friends or enemies able to pull me back.*

"Gary?"

"Yeah?"

"What would you say was needed above all else to achieve the *Képi Blanc?"* (The *Képi Blanc* is the symbolic white cap received upon acceptance into the *Légion*.)

"Desperation!"

I laughed. "Desperation is all I've got."

I started reading books about the *Légion*, and it was astonishing to read the stories of men throughout history who had joined. The promise of a new identity and a fresh start; the possibility of "belonging" again, and perhaps regaining some honour, sent my heart beating. It was clear that the possibility of a fresh start had the power to transform rejects, renegades, and heinous criminals into serious soldiers. The *Légion* offered an opportunity for men to change, but at a great price. Yet for so many, the opportunity was not only worth fighting for, but dying for...

As I considered all this, I wondered if this was what I was really looking for in Christ – a new identity and a forgotten past. Anyway, I determined to give this "Jesus thing" a go. I had decided before leaving HMP Edinburgh that I would attend every church service possible, with the intention of finding out more about what it meant to "follow" Christ. I had no clue what that meant, but I wanted to carry this through. So on Monday mornings I attended an Episcopalian Bible study run by a very kindly lady called Fiánach. On Tuesday afternoons I met with some Christians doing restorative justice groups and Alpha courses. On Wednesday mornings I went to the Catholic mass, and on Thursday evenings I attended the Prison Fellowship meetings. Finally, on Friday afternoons I attended the Church of Scotland service. Anything offering Jesus I went to. Unfortunately the chaplains had other Sunday obligations, otherwise my weekends would have included attending more services.

The screws became very suspicious of me running off to every service. Although I believed I was doing "the Christian thing" by attending every service I could, I still saw no problem in organizing my own personal supply of cannabis and in ensuring I'd taken the necessary measures to have a comfortable time within the jail. This is easily done when drugs are acquired. For the smallest amount of dope, I would be able to stock my supplies of juice, sweets, crisps, shower gels, and shaving foam – all that represented the prison's currency. As long as I was not stabbing or slashing anyone, surely God didn't mind a "wee bit of coming and going"? Furthermore, my mates on the outside were still punting a lot of gear and they offered to bring, or arrange for me to have, all that I needed within Glenochil. Quite satisfied with my comfortable little plan to get away from violence, I saw no disparity in going along and enjoying a bit of church too.

"Where you going, Gielty?" asked one angry screw, opening my cell after the Prison Fellowship service had been announced down the wing.

"To church!" I replied.

"Who are you kidding?" mocked another. "We're watching you."

"We're watching you?" I mocked right back. "God forbid any one of us should try and better ourselves! If we do, it's good to know you'll be right there to discourage it."

"We'll see, Gielty."

"You will see," I assured them.

Their suspicions were well founded, as the chaplaincy department was frequently the target for smuggling and drug exchanges because of its position in the prison system. It was one of the only places where multiple wings could converge, thus making transitions easy. Wearied chaplains welcomed souls from every wing, knowing that this convergence created a congregation of prisoners who would capitalize on the trust the chaplains themselves had fought to bring us. Yet, in the hope of change, they risked betrayal and we, like a bunch of Judases, betrayed them. Undoubtedly this contributed to the look of defeat and dejection imprinted on so many of the chaplains' faces. They were labouring among people so entrenched within a culture of criminality that true change required nothing less than the intervention of the God they believed in.

Despite my blind hypocrisy, my spirit was thirsting for God, and I longed to speak with the "people of God".

I came up against several difficulties, however, when trying to seek direction from some of the chaplains. One was their lack of time, which made obtaining significant spiritual direction impossible. The chaplains were just so busy. Despite their sincerity and care, many just seemed so preoccupied with getting through their "list". This is a difficult and unfortunate consequence of a packed prison population that leaves chaplains stretched. Priests, ministers, and laity alike not only have the prison to worry about, but their parishes too, resulting in an often inevitable superficiality in the prison's pastoral care.

Another troubling difficulty was that there were many liberal chaplains who, when I attempted to speak with them about God or the things of God, often seemed a little uncomfortable. They would change the subject quickly, as if they were slightly embarrassed and as if God just wasn't acceptable. They steered the conversation away from him through jokes or discussions about current affairs. Others among the chaplains had lost their way completely, and would be effing and blinding in the course of their conversations with us. Rather than making us feel they were one of the lads as they hoped, it actually distanced them from us. One chaplain even informed me that he didn't think it was a problem that I was smoking weed! We needed them to help us to find God – we were dying for lack of knowledge. We did not need another "one of the lads" but rather a light to help bring us out of our darkness.

***

Before I left HMP Edinburgh, Fr John told me, "You're going to meet a saint."

"Eh?" I replied.

"Her name's Patricia."

He just left it at that, leaving me somewhat confused. But sure enough, a few weeks into my time at Glenochil, I was introduced to this Patricia, who would become the voice of one crying out in our wilderness.

"Hi Patricia, Fr John McFadden told me to say hello."

It has been said that "One of the rarest and purest forms of generosity is to pay attention" (Simone Weil). It was this type of generosity that distinguished Patricia Roberts from all the other chaplains, because when she talked with us she made us feel that we were important enough to be heard. Patricia's gentleness within the harsh prison environment stood out like a flower within a concrete wall: it was precisely its delicateness that made people pay attention. Yet this gentleness drew attention to itself only to point beyond itself, to its author. Like a living signpost, she always directed us to Christ. Her spirit was on fire with the love of God and it shone from her in so many ways that the cons had to confess that there was "something different about her". Or, as one con put it in the negative sense, "No one should be that nice." Such was Patricia's witness.

Every time I spoke to Patricia I got the sense that something amazing was about to happen. Patricia did not serve a dead God or a philosophical ideal; she revealed a God who was alive, who cared, a God who brought colour and life into the grey prison and greyer prisoners. She seemed to know a God who wasn't confined to visit times, but who could cut through razor wire and crack stone walls as well as stone hearts. The most compelling thing about her God was that He did not represent society's views: He was a "friend of sinners".

"Anthony, I think you'd love this book on St Louis-Marie de Montfort."

"Who's that?" I asked, thinking the name sounded a bit girly.

"He's the saint who's had me by the scruff of the neck, both challenging and inspiring me to do God's will," she laughed.

"What?" I replied.

"Take a look," she said, handing me a copy of a book called *Wisdom's Fool.*

"Wisdom's Fool," I read aloud. "What's it called that for?"

She then went on to tell me how this French saint called Louis de Montfort loved to refer to Jesus Christ as "Wisdom Incarnate," since "Jesus Christ is the very Wisdom of the Father, through whom God created everything and by whom He holds all things together." She told me excitedly that I could "find all this in Proverbs 8, John 1 and Colossians 1". It was clear she knew a lot about this Louis guy and the Bible, but I was thinking, *What on earth is she talking about? She even refers to this saint like she knows him too: "Louis loved to refer to Jesus as…" eh?*

So, as she continued, "He is the image of the unseen…" I nodded, as if I clearly understood all that she was saying, and I told her, "I'll check it out."

I wasn't really expecting very much from it, but out of respect for Patricia, I would read it.

8

Behold, I Stand at the Door and Knock

HMP Glenochil

As I lay back on my bed and began to read the story of the saint Patricia loved so well, I was drawn into the world of St Louis-Marie de Montfort...

It is a still night, only a few lights flicker as families and homes rest in the tranquil French town of Dinan. Then, there is an echo of footsteps on the road, the sound of the strides denotes purpose, intention, a sense of mission. Accompanying the regular rhythm of his steps there can be heard the faint but familiar sound of a Rosary, brushing off the person as he moves quickly on. The silhouette of a powerfully built man can be traced through the shadows. Sharp features, accentuated in the dim moonlight, a long roman nose and a stubborn chin. Suddenly, this wayfarer's attention is drawn to the shadows; he stops instantly. Without hesitation he moves over to the body of a man lying in the darkness. The man on the ground feebly tries to hide away. The sight and smell of the man, with his face gnawed and twisted, had made everyone that saw him steer clear. Yet, rather than repulse this wayfarer, it seems to draw him closer. He is a leper. For all this wayfarer's powerful characteristics, his most distinguishing quality is tenderness. Then, mirroring another man that touched lepers, he tenderly consoles the pitiful man and picks him up in his arms and carries him. The swift stride of the man moving through the sleepy town becomes even more intentional. As he reaches the mission house he finds it locked. Then, with the roar of a prophet, this powerful yet tender man cries out, in a call that has woken the dead in many centuries...

"OPEN THE DOOR... OPEN THE DOOR TO JESUS CHRIST!" The sleepy doorkeeper bolts upright and rushes to open the door. Fr Louis Grignion de Montfort steps through the threshold; amidst protest and scandal he insists this deformed, mutilated man have his own bed.

(Papasogli, *Montfort: A Prophet for Our Times,* author's
paraphrase)

St Louis de Montfort spoke to me with a force of tenderness and a compassion so compelling that I would never look at Christ or His church in the same way again. There was just something so disturbing about it all now.

This saint knew something I did not, something so real, so true, something so worth living for, but what? He lived as though God was real; moreover, his life seemed to show that God was behind him. I couldn't wait to speak with Patricia the following week, and within a couple of days I finished the book on Montfort's life she had given me. I had so many questions about this guy Louis-Marie that it made waiting for the Wednesday Mass almost impossible.

Deeply intrigued by this man and fascinated by the life he had lived, I was hooked. It represented *true* courage and *true* fearlessness, which stood in such stark contrast to my definitions of those virtues. The son of a lawyer, St Louis was born in Montfort-la-Cane in Brittany, France, on 31 January 1673. He was educated by the Jesuits at the college of St Thomas Becket at Rennes for eight years. Then, called to study for the priesthood in Paris at the age of twenty, he set out from Brittany. Embracing evangelical poverty, he walked the 200-mile journey on foot, begging as he went and sharing all he had with the poor. He took the words of Jesus seriously: "Take nothing for your journey" and "Do not be anxious about your life, what you will eat or what you will drink, nor about your body, what you will put on..." (Luke 9:3; Matthew 6:25).

Arriving in Paris, he took up his studies at St Sulpice and the Sorbonne University. He stood out because of his intellectual ability, excessive love of God, and tender love of the poor. He was ordained a priest in 1700 and longed to go the French colonies to spread the gospel. This desire was an indication that, as a young boy instructed by the Jesuits (who would remain a pillar of strength for him when all others turned him away), their faith had captivated him through the stories of their Jesuit brothers labouring to bring the light of Christ to the Americas. Undoubtedly, the stories of the North American martyrs who had suffered terrible deaths in evangelizing the Huron, Mohawk, and Iroquois Indians had reached Louis, stories like those of Jean de Brébeuf and Gabriel Lallement.

As I thought of how these martyrs had inspired St Louis, again I remembered the martyr stories that Mrs Peterson had told us in school, stories of St Andrew, and of those who had walked bravely out to meet their fate in the Roman arenas, and how they had inspired me as a child. I had devoured the books she had given me on Louis, so Patricia began to give me books on the lives of such saints and martyrs, and I began to read some of the very stories that would have inspired Louis himself.

The shocking stories of those willing to give everything to share the gospel greatly challenged my lifeless, causeless, selfish existence. In stark comparison, these men had a cause they believed in – a cause of love, and not hate. They were willing to suffer horrific martyrdoms even for the people they were trying to reach. Their stories, along with the countless other narratives of love evidenced in the lives of the saints, shook me.

Although Louis' life had not ended in martyrdom, I marvelled at the martyrdom of self-denial he endured every day of his life. He encountered years of opposition because of his uncompromising commitment to the gospel, and was commanded many times to leave parishes, churches, and dioceses following insult, rebuke, humiliation, and all manner of persecutions, including being poisoned. After all this, his heart was, as Fr Besnard, an early biographer, said, "squeezed like a sponge, yet it could not release a drop of bitterness". Louis and the other martyrs were willing to turn the other cheek when they faced hatred. This was a foreign concept within the gang culture that I was used to, yet it pulled me in further and further, redefining more of my perverse perspectives on justice, bravery, and loyalty.

Yet St Louis was no helpless victim or soft target. He was swift to challenge injustice wherever he found it, and his outspoken denunciation of that which was wrong led him to walk the lonely road reserved for those possessed of God alone. I shuddered at the challenge of this. Again, my life stood in such stark contrast to his. Here was a man willing to give up everything he had to serve the poor in obedience to Jesus, while I only served myself by exploiting the poor and vulnerable. Here was a man willing to give up everything for what he believed in, while I was living only for the moment and for personal gain.

St Louis' life and testimony seemed so radical that I began to doubt whether it was possible even for a "normal" person to imitate him, let alone someone with a mind as depraved as mine. I recalled from one of Patricia's books on the saint that Louis had been questioned along the same lines by one of his early companions. This man had asked whether such a life was not reserved for a chosen few. But Louis simply reached for his New Testament and asked his questioner if he could see anything wrong with what Jesus had said and done, and whether the life Louis was leading was close to that of Christ or not.

Louis had remained steadfast in his commitment to living as Jesus lived and giving all he had to help others. As I read on, though, I realized he had his struggles. Eventually, wounded by so much criticism, so many setbacks and hurts, he began to wonder if he was following God's path. After being expelled from yet another diocese, he began to question whether his time and energy would be put to better use on the mission field of the New France. He decided that there was only one way to settle it, and so he set out for HQ, as only Louis could. He walked more than a thousand miles to Rome and put the matter to the Pope himself. In June 1706, Clement XI informed him that France "contained enough scope for his zeal" and sent him back, but this time with the title "Missionary Apostolic". The Holy Father had given him the green light and was sending him back as his very own champion of orthodoxy to the land threatened with a host of heresies.

Louis therefore continued his ministry for some time, never relaxing his austerity or poverty. However, after being poisoned by some of his opponents, his health would never be the same again. Though he continued to preach and teach, finally his strength gave way. After giving his last sermon, on "the tenderness of Jesus" he became gravely ill. On his deathbed he cried out, "In vain do you attack me. I am between Jesus and Mary. I have finished my course, all is over. I shall sin no more." His epitaph reads:

> *A priest of Christ, he showed forth Christ in*
> *his actions, and preached him everywhere*
> *in his words. Tireless, he rested only in the*
> *grave. Father of the poor, protector of orphans,*
> *reconciler of sinners, his glorious death was the*
> *image of his life: as he lived, so he died, ripe for*
> *God...*

Here was a true "go-ahead", someone who truly did what he thought was right, no matter how it was perceived. The life of Montfort served as such an evidence for God.

I kept repeating over and over in my mind, *No man could live this way unless they knew God. How is it that anyone could be so set on God unless they were absolutely convinced of God's existence?* Furthermore, all that was attractive about the French Foreign Legion – the guts, the glory – was now totally blown away by this Frenchman and the standard he set for transforming one's life.

I found no trace of serving the ego in the life of St Louis-Marie de Montfort. Here was a man doing what was right to his own hurt, for his God and love of his neighbour. His tenderness, consistency, and inability to compromise demonstrated that Montfort was ablaze with the love of Jesus. This authenticity drove me to discover more.

"Hey, Patricia," I greeted her at our next meeting. "I've finished those books you gave me," and I handed back the stack of books I had devoured.

"Already?" she asked, looking surprised that I had read them so fast.

"Yeah, they blew me away," I replied. "I just can't get over Montfort."

"That reminds me," said Patricia. "I have a small book written by St Louis. I think that in it you'll discover more of Montfort's love for Jesus."

"Awesome. I'd love to read it."

I was excited to be getting to know more of what this man practised and taught. We continued to talk for a while about Louis and his life, as well as the lives of the saints and the martyrs I had read about. Then, wanting to understand why their stories had caught my attention so greatly, I turned to Patricia and asked, "What is it about the saints that makes them so beautiful?"

"It's the communion of saints, Anthony. That's what is so important!" she replied.

"What do you mean?"

"I mean the communion of saints is incredible," she continued. "The amazing thing is that, as Catholics, we recognize that the saints are more alive now than they ever were. Consequently, they are of tremendous help to us."

"What do you mean, like in heaven?" I asked.

"Yes, exactly," she continued, her face lighting up as she spoke. "The Catholic Church is not just something confined to here and now. It goes beyond all you can imagine. You really are part of something so special, Anthony."

"Eh?" I was still confused.

"Yes, the Church is incredible," she went on. "It exists in three states: the Church Militant, the Church Expectant, and the Church Triumphant. My friend who is an Augustinian..."

"What's that?" I interjected.

"He's a monk who follows the monastic rule of St Augustine. Anyway, before I was a Catholic, my friend..."

"You weren't always a Catholic?" I interrupted again, surprised that this saintly woman could ever have been anything but steeped in that which she was sharing with me so clearly.

"No, I'm a convert," she stated. "Anyway, my Augustinian friend at one point had to explain to me a little of what the Catholic Church is and what it represents. It really is wonderful. The Church Militant represents us, in the midst of the struggle here on earth, fighting for God against the devil, the world, and the flesh. The Church Expectant are those who, having died in Christ, are en route to heaven through further purification; and The Church Triumphant are all the saints throughout all time who are in heaven right now, interceding for us before the throne of Christ. Because of this, the Body of Christ – that is, the Catholic Church – consequently exists as one family in three states until the last day."

"This is blowing my mind," I said, trying to get my head round all she had just explained.

"It blew my mind too," she responded. "But you need to know you really are part of something so special. That's why it's so important to understand the communion of saints. As you read about the lives of the saints and martyrs, be assured that they're not just fairy tales or dead historical figures. They are part of the same fellowship as us. The only difference is that they are experiencing now what we will experience in the future, and from that blessed state they are able to assist us here."

"Assist us how?" I asked.

"Basically, they are like our older brothers and sisters, who we can ask to pray for us. They are strong intercessors since they participate in the beatific vision."

"The what?" I said, quite involuntarily.

"You know how you can ask someone to pray for you here on earth? Well, you can also ask the saints to intercede for you in heaven, since they see God face to face. Basically, St Louis is more alive now than he ever was because he is *alive to God!* It was after reading the writings of Teresa of Avila, a wonderful Spanish saint, that I made up my mind to become Catholic. Her love for Jesus inspired me to give my life to Him through the Catholic Church."

"Wow!" I was astounded, even though I didn't understand it all. Patricia had just gone off on one: she just gets very excited and has to share it all, but I was so glad she had.

This is so exciting, I thought. *Although I don't really believe, well maybe I do... Well, I don't know... It's pretty cool stuff, and being part of the Church Militant means I'm already part of something really significant.* I was smiling as I thought about not having to join the *Légion Étrangère* for a fresh start. I chuckled to myself unintentionally.

"You look happy, Anthony," came Patricia's voice, jolting me back to reality. I was daydreaming about it all, and had forgotten that I was in a conversation with Patricia.

"Eh? Sorry," I muttered, looking sheepishly at my feet. "It's... it's... it's just really exciting," I stuttered, looking up at her, and then, feeling embarrassed at my declaration, I thought, *I can't believe I said that about church.*

"I know," she said. "It's wonderful." She smiled at me, without a hint of sarcasm. "Anyway, I'll bring you in some more books," she said as she got up to leave.

"Oh, and the book by Louis please," I quickly put in.

"Don't worry, I'll remember," she replied.

I began to smile as I thought about the *Légion* again, and I laughed as my mind drew a comparison between the French Foreign Legion and the Church Militant, described by Patricia as an army. *Both take care of your past,* I thought, *one temporally and one eternally. One offers new citizenship on earth, the other citizenship in heaven; both are made up of all nations; both offer new identities, though yet again, one temporally, one eternally.* I recalled the words of one kind chaplain, known as "American Bob", who had told me, " 'If anyone is in Christ, he is a new creation. The old has passed away; behold, the new has come' (2 Corinthians 5:17). You get a new start, man, the old is gone!"

It wasn't long before Patricia brought me more

books, including, as promised, the little book by Montfort. From Fr John to Patricia and now St Louis de Montfort, I couldn't believe how interested I was becoming in it all.

***

"It was through the Blessed Virgin Mary that Jesus Christ came into the world…"

With these words, Montfort begins his book, *True Devotion*. Then, drawing his authority from Scripture, the voice of the church, and personal conviction, he points to Mary's role as the vehicle through which God the Father chose to give us His only begotten Son. Sharpening his focus still further on the incarnation, Montfort demonstrates that it was in Mary, and through Mary, that the Holy Spirit performed His "masterpiece" – that is, the forming of the God–Man, Jesus Christ.

Through St Louis de Montfort's teachings I came to see the importance of Mary's role. Furthermore, because I had come to know something of St Louis' life, witness, and authenticity, the teaching carried authority. Therefore, I immediately took Montfort's advice and began to say the Rosary every day. In consequence, I began to have deep experiences of peace that lingered long into my days. I did not understand any of it; all I knew was that when I prayed the Rosary, peace followed, as did a deeper love of Jesus and a longing for Him. Whenever my cellmate was out, I would be saying it. I would say it slyly under my covers at night, too. Incredibly, I began to experience more and more peace. I wasn't even sure that I was saying it correctly, but I just kept saying my Hail Marys and mediating on the Gospels until I felt that unparalleled peace within the very pit of my stomach, which had formerly been mostly a place of angst and pain.

9

Crossroads

HMP Glenochil

In Plato's work *Phaedrus,* Socrates compares the soul to a chariot being led by two winged horses. The charioteer driving it seeks a glimpse of heaven – the realm of the divine, the place of everlasting truth and beauty, where justice and knowledge reside. However, the two winged horses pulling the chariot have stark differences in both appearance and temperaments. One is light and the other dark. The white horse continually pulls upward toward heaven, is noble and determined to move up and be nourished by the things above. The dark horse, however, is obstinate, rebellious, and intent on pulling the chariot down to the realm of the base.

Plato's ancient analogy portrays the struggle of the soul attempting to move upward to the eternal good, but no matter how hard the white horse of noble intention strives upward, man always finds the dark horse of his passions and destructive inclinations pulling him furiously downward. All the while the charioteer, representing reason, tries desperately to prevent the chariot from being ripped apart. So it was with all my "good intentions" and efforts to strive toward higher and nobler ends, that I very suddenly felt the downward pull of my dark side.

***

"It's a miracle, Tony," said the excited officer. Three screws had taken me into the supervisor's office.

"What is?" I questioned, wearily expecting bad news despite the happy tone.

"It's been six months and you have not been in a single fight," said another screw.

"Whatever you've been doing, it's working," added another in a more cynical tone. "No stabbings or slashings; nothing – not even a scrap."

"A miracle," repeated the first screw in earnest.

The supervisor gestured for us to sit down, and said, "Tony, we want to commend you for what you're doing. It's just great to see the change in you."

Then they got round to why I was really there. "Your friend Matt Webster, who has just started his eleven-year stretch in Polmont, is already going off the rails. He's involved in many attacks in Polmont, and we know he's your friend. He's wasting away in solitary, just *like you were*." He emphasized the last part, letting me know he knew about Polmont and what I had gone through there. "What we are asking is, if you think it's a good idea to bring him up here beside you? Then perhaps some of the good things that are happening in your life might rub off on him."

I paused for a moment to consider this. They were genuinely impressed that I had gone six months in HMP Glenochil without a fight. But I doubted they really cared for a prisoner in Polmont. What they wanted to know was whether or not trouble would hit them if he came here.

My thoughts then turned to myself, and I wondered whether or not I really wanted someone who knew the old me to enter this environment where I was trying to lose an unwanted reputation. Here, I had peace for the first time in so long. Matt's arrival would undoubtedly bring an unspoken pressure to conform to the old ways. I mean, I was now attending church services! I did not need the reports filtering back to Edinburgh that I was a "Bible Basher". I had tried to hide myself from it all and just enjoy the fellowships, and with them the new friends, who cared nothing for reputations and who placed no burdens or expectations on me.

Bitterly, I realized my past would not be outrun: it was now rushing straight toward me. Matt would bring his attitude with him – the same attitude I was slowly losing – and with it would come the old mentality, the old rules, then shortly after that, new troubles. I could say no, warn them of all this, betray my old rules to save myself, and inform the screws that trouble would surely come of this. But how could I? I had never spoken thus to screws or ever sought for them to make my life easier. How could I bear the thought of anyone being left in the tombs of Polmont while I reinvented myself and fled the old gang rules? I could not endure the thought of anyone languishing in Polmont.

"Bring him here; this is a great opportunity. He will be fine," I lied, and walked out of the office and back on to the wing, wondering how long it would be before Matt arrived, and with him my shadows.

***

Matt arrived on the wing and it was like watching a car crash in slow motion. *This will only end one way,* I thought. I watched him from across the section as he swaggered down the landing, with a bag containing his possessions over his shoulder. Before entering his cell he had already started arguing with screws and was refusing to go in. It seemed I was looking at myself just six months earlier, and I knew then that I had changed. I was not condemning Matt, only observing the same old attitudes I had once demonstrated. Through fellowship, however, and reading God's word, and especially through receiving the Eucharist, changes were being wrought in me, though I still had a very long way to go.

I walked over and welcomed him. "Hey, Matt."

"Tony, how you doing?"

"Really good to see you," I said.

"Right, see these?" he spat, pointing at the screws. "They think I'm a bam, but I've warned them not to treat me like one." And Matt started to hurl obscenities at the screws, spitting curses at them – the overflow of a hating and hurting heart. Matt was raging because not all his property had arrived at the wing yet. I explained to him that the delay was likely to be because it was still being processed, and not because the screws thought he was an idiot.

I cringed as I watched Matt argue with many cons and screws alike, back and forth, trying to get the last word in. He always had to be right, and was desperate to prove himself, to ensure that no one would treat him disrespectfully. Suddenly I began to understand why my life had been such a violent mess. I saw through Matt's actions that it was really lads like us who were the problem. There was a prevailing mindset within the gang culture that ensured we would remain trapped within our hostile, angry, and aggressive attitudes. This said mindset, if not understood and addressed, would continue to leave a trail of devastation in its wake.

So it happened. As I walked into the barber's, I noticed Matt sitting in the seat prepped for a haircut, but nobody was cutting his hair. The atmosphere was icy. Matt was growling into the mirror at the reflection of a group of men standing behind him. One guy was tightly holding a long pair of scissors in a threatening manner. It turned out all the hairdressers were refusing to cut Matt's hair, since Matt had fought one of the barber's family members back in Polmont. Matt was outnumbered and not tooled up, so I instinctively stepped between the men.

"Put the scissors away or I'll bury you here."

"What's this to you, Tony?" one of them said.

"That's one of my troops."

"Fine," said Brad, the one with the grievance. "But it's not over."

"So let's settle this on the wing tonight," I responded.

"Good," said Brad.

Back on the wing, this particular con was connected to several gangsters from Glasgow. One of them was John MacDonagh, a well-known "hard man". They would undoubtedly pull many men to themselves, so we had to think this through. Matt and I talked as we returned to the wing, planning secretly as we marched in twos along a line numbering hundreds of prisoners. I was then locked in my cell to await dinner. Whereas previously the anticipation of violence had been my daily bread and I consumed it unperturbed, secretly hoping to rush into a cell and be killed, now it was different. Hope had come to me along the way. I had enjoyed the peace of seeking God and dreaming of another way. I had been learning about Jesus and, more than anything, I wanted to follow him and imitate Montfort.

I knew this would happen. Why now? Just when I thought my life would change. I'll tell Matt he needs to wise up, grow up, stop acting like a punk, and start treating himself and others with respect. I am going God's way now.

But then my thoughts would go the other way...

Listen to yourself! If I don't back Matt up, people will think I'm going soft. All the troops back in Edinburgh will hear of this and I'll be disgraced.

The inner turmoil continued as I sat on the bed. I had come to the crossroads. I had to choose between the way of blessing demonstrated in non-violence by Christ and the church, or continue on the path of hatred and violence. One path would bring peace, but it would also bring shame in the eyes of men. The other path would bring the honour of men, and shame in the eyes of God.

I gave way to cowardice and consented to the praise of men. I could not endure the thought of being looked upon as weak. I would go forth to back Matt up and stab to death anyone who would oppose us.

My cell was opened for dinner. The atmosphere on the wing was growing in intensity. I collected my meal and sat down at my table, watching carefully. I was joined by Justin and Matt as well as several other mates from Glasgow and others from Paisley.

"How's this going to go down?" asked Justin.

"At recreation, we'll kick this off," I said.

"I've already put two large batteries in a football sock. I'll smash their skulls in," said Rob.

"Have they got blades?" asked Matt.

"Do you really want to know?" I replied.

"I need to know," said Matt.

"Well, I'll tell you the truth bluntly: they'll be tooled to the back teeth – and not so bluntly." I let out a ragged manic laugh, which made some of the men at the table look at me strangely.

"But I don't have a tool!" Matt said, looking at me expectantly.

"Do you know that twenty-one lockback knives were found hanging off the razor wire a couple of weeks ago? The bag got caught in the fence as someone tried to throw it over. The screws were in uproar. They were found on the wire next to Harvestoun Wing."

"How long have they been smuggling those parcels in?" asked Matt.

"Who knows?" I shrugged. "Don't worry, I've got a nice tool for you."

***

Within hours, Matt had been attacked. The choice before me was clear: whether or not to avenge my mate, as I was required to do. I had the weapon, and I had John McDonagh with his back to me: I just had to get on with it.

I glanced at Matt and froze. What I was looking at paralysed me. Matt was staring straight at me with his palms opened. They were pierced. The bandage I had wrapped around the crown of his head was now soaked with blood, and because of the way it had been tied, his hair spiked up with sweat and bloody matter, forming a ragged crown. His body was also punctured. He looked so much like Jesus with His pierced hands, wounded body, and crown of thorns, I was stunned. It was my mate Matt, not a vision or hallucination; it was Matt, clear as day, yet he looked so much like Christ in that moment. That strange resemblance served as a living icon and stopped me, then and there, from savagely stabbing a man to death.

10

Come Back to Me

HMP Glenochil

After the stabbing, the wing was instantly put on lockdown. Officers poured onto the landing like regimented ants and began shoving grumbling prisoners into their cells and slamming steel doors shut. I was not in my cell for long before the screws came back to take me to the Seg Unit. The cameras had been checked and I, along with everyone else suspected of having the slightest involvement or information, were taken to isolation for investigation.

Within the Seg cell, confusion and hatred churned. The seething cauldron of my mind bubbled with rage that was about to spill everywhere. I was on the cusp of returning to the path of violence that I had been trying to leave behind. The image of the blood-drenched face and body of Matt was seared into my memory. His voice pleading for me to take revenge swirled around inside my head, causing me to pace my cell back and forth like a tormented animal, cornered and trapped but restlessly pacing, in the vain hope that movement might bring relief. There was no relief. Had I, through my own naivety, just allowed my friend to be killed? Was I becoming too vulnerable through all this Christian stuff? Where was God, "the Almighty", in all this? *In Polmont, they wouldn't see me coming; I'd have a razor across their faces at the first hint of tension.*

The words that had been drummed into me since I was a kid were, "Be first, Tony, be first." First to slip the jab, first to take the centre of the ring, first to finish the fight. In prison, this "be first" became about ensuring I was the first to strike. I had never ever paused, never trusted, and now, perceiving myself to be in grievous error, I wanted to scream out in frustration. How could I have been so stupid? I had rejected everything I had ever known, and in consequence I had lost the perfect opportunity for revenge.

I had him on a plate: all I had to do was put my screwdriver through his neck and he was dead, I thought, as I paced my cell in frustration. Yet seconds later, I stopped sharply as I recalled the reason why I had not opened up John's neck. Chills ran up my spine as my mind's eye brought forth the image of Matt's pierced hands and body and the blood-soaked bandage wrapped around the crown of his head. All pierced and bleeding, he had looked so much like Jesus – just like the picture on my gran's wall that we used to see when we visited her. I had been a split second from killing John and I had looked at Matt to make sure he could savour the moment I dropped his enemy. But Matt had looked so much like Jesus that I couldn't do it.

Why has this happened now? I questioned sharply. *Why now?* I refused to call out to God – this was His fault! After all, I had been attending every fellowship and church meeting the prison had to offer and now, in spite of all my efforts, He had allowed this to happen! Now I would certainly be put on the Ghost Train. Moreover, I would have to call my family and, having already declared myself to be a changed man, once again I would have to explain that I was back in the digger. I could already picture the call: "Yeah, that's me back down again, Mum. Oh, and don't worry, your son's not a total headcase, by the way!"

I began to fill up with poisonous words that I wanted to hurl at God, urged on by some impulse demanding I spit these venomous curses in heaven's direction. Yet at the very moment I went to spew forth my torrent of abuse, I stopped and knelt down on the cold cell floor and whispered, "Lord, have mercy."

I arose more confused than ever. I had wanted to accuse God horribly, yet deep below my black rage was a still, small voice, bruised but not broken; there was a smouldering flame, not entirely snuffed out, faintly longing for the light of God. This little voice broke through the pain and pride, surfacing just in time to muzzle a beast before it could insult its creator. With all these confused thoughts spinning round in my head, I drifted into a troubled night's sleep.

"You want exercise?" came my rude awakening as the screws battered on the door.

"Aye," I said sleepily, waking up.

The screws were standing at my cell door impatiently. My eyelids were like lead. I was shattered. It had been a long night of tossing and turning, with heaps of unanswered questions. I needed some air, and if exercise was not taken when offered, it would be another twenty-four hours before another opportunity came around.

"Let's go then," I barked at the screw.

It took every effort to pick myself up, and when I got outside, it was all a blur. My mind kept returning to the events of the day before. I wished it had all been a dream, wondering if it were possible to be woken up from a hellish existence.

No, this isn't a dream. This is your life, and it's rubbish, came the voice in my head. *Get used to it!*

The library was at my door when I returned. The "library" consisted of three shelves on wheels with a random assortment of books stacked upon them, which would be wheeled round the cells from time to time. Seizing the opportunity, as I knew I would be in the digger for a while, I grabbed three books. The first was a book on animals, called *The Intelligence of Animals*. I had liked animals since I was a kid, so I thought this would help me pass the time. The next book I noticed, and went for instinctively, was the Bible. It was in my hand when I noticed the three screws staring at me. Instantly I felt ashamed, as reading the Bible could be perceived as a sign of weakness. Nevertheless, I kept it in my hand and then, in an attempt to smother my religious leanings and recover some "cred", I swiftly grabbed the nearest gangster book I could find: a book about the mafia and the JFK assassination, called *Double Cross*.

As soon as I was locked in my cell, the pacing began again. Back and forth; back and forth. There was still no word on how Matt was, and the questions concerning this awful situation continued. *What's happening on the wing? Did they find my stash of weapons? Has anything else kicked off? What's happened to my mate?*

Where is your God now? came the cold, familiar voice, tightening its coils of doubt and despair.

I looked over at the Bible I had picked up earlier and noticed that there was a page folded over, perhaps by some reader from years earlier, in a book called Amos. I had never even heard of such a name, never mind known it was in the Bible. Immediately my attention was drawn to verses 6 to 12 of chapter 4, where the page was creased. Then, as if Israel's situation and Amos' prophecy somehow corresponded to me, these words from the passage leapt out as I read them:

"Still you did not come back to me..." (v8)

"Still you did not come back to me..." (v9)

"I killed your young men in battle... Still you did not come back to me..." (v10)

Suddenly, at the very moment my eyes met the words of verse 11 "Still you did not...", a screw walked past my door and sang, "COME BACK TO ME"! At that precise moment! No one could have timed it with such perfect accuracy. I froze, shocked to the core. My astonishment held me breathless. Then, cautiously, I let my eyes return to this "strange book".

As I continued and my eyes met with verse 12, my horrified heart twisted within me as I read the words, "Get ready to face my judgment!"

Fear and trembling gripped me in a way I had never experienced before. This was too real. I slammed the Bible shut and started panicking. But I was unable to stay away from it. It terrified me, yet it pulled me back to itself. I quickly opened it up again and read through the entire book of Amos. I devoured it, desperately trying to understand its content. Though it was a simple enough, illustrated Good News Bible, its language and concepts were still foreign. However, the prophet hammered into my soul the condemnation of hypocrisy. Amos railed against the hypocrisy of a people claiming to be okay with God, yet underneath their religious exterior they were exploiting the poor and outraging God with their sins.

It was as if the prophet had me in mind as he proclaimed his message, and the more I read, the more I trembled. My awareness of my own injustice and uncleanness became stronger and stronger. My soul began to buckle under the weight of God's truth, His holiness exposing my vileness. For years pangs of conscience had assailed me in relation to my deeds done to others, but now, for the first time, a sharp awareness of the weight of my offences against God was brought forth. I had stood in the highest court of my country, in front of the highest representatives of my nation's law, but that was as child's play in comparison to the thought of the judgment of God. I sensed acutely that my soul was being summoned to give an account of itself before the judge of all the earth. No facade, no aggression, no argument or deception could deflect His holy gaze. There was nowhere to run.

> *"Even if they dig their way down to the world of*
> *the dead, I will catch them. Even if they climb*
> *up to heaven, I will bring them down... If they*
> *are taken into captivity by their enemies, I will*

order them to be put to death. I am determined
to destroy them, not to help them."

Amos 9:2, 4 (GNB)

Amos rose up as God's powerful prosecutor who, with deadly force, was driving home the charges of injustice, uncleanness, and hypocrisy with horrifying accuracy. Although I had been attending every church meeting, both Protestant and Catholic, during those six months after having met with Fr John in HMP Edinburgh, all my church attendance and hymn singing was revealed as unpleasing, even repugnant, to God.

The Lord says, "I hate your religious festivals; I
cannot stand them... Stop your noisy songs; I do
not want to listen to your harps."

Amos 5:21, 23 (GNB)

Yesterday I had wanted to accuse God on the basis of my own righteousness, my church attendance and pious dedication. I now remembered that I had attended those gatherings of men and women of God while being stoned out of my face, and that at times I had made things difficult for the leaders, asking awkward questions, constantly criticizing and finding fault with their churches, their Bible, and their answers.

You people hate anyone who challenges
injustice and speaks the whole truth.

Amos 5:10 (GNB)

All that I had previously seen as "pious dedication" was seen for what it was: "disgusting rags". More than this, the whole time I had been claiming to be a disciple of Jesus Christ, I was in contact, via my smuggled-in mobile phone, with my friends involved in organized crime. Through our actions, we did indeed "trample on the needy and try to destroy the poor of the country" (Amos 8:4, GNB). All through this time that I had been professing Christ, I'd had clothing, money, and other possessions handed in to prison, the fruit of the addict, "slaves" that were bought and sold for the price of "a pair of sandals" (Amos 8:6, GNB), by my mates who "fill their mansions with things taken by crime and violence" (Amos 3:10, GNB). This prophet knew too much; his attacks on injustice were relentless.

I could not bear it any longer. On every page the voice of God roared through the ages, from the eighth century BC right into my cell in May 2006: "I know how terrible your sins are and how many crimes you have committed" (Amos 5:12, GNB).

This book was alive! I slammed it shut and wanted to run from it as far as I could. But there was no place to run. It seemed that the hand of God had dragged me down to this point and was not willing to let me go.

"If He wants me to read it, I will," I thought. I opened the Bible in the New Testament, what I thought would be a safe distance from Amos! But my eyes fell at once on the Scripture, "It is impossible to bring them back to repent again, because they are again crucifying the Son of God and exposing him to public shame" (Hebrews 6:6, GNB). My heart was paralysed by these words. I was convinced that this text spoke directly into my hypocrisy, that through my actions I had abandoned my faith and now, in consequence, it was "impossible" for me to be forgiven. Thoughts and images of all my sins flooded my mind, things that my closest friends and family would never have expected, not even from a criminal. Even things that I had long forgotten, despite my years of self-examination and self-hatred, filled my every thought. My life was an abomination, and I shuddered as I became even more aware of my filthiness.

Then one disgusting sin raised its head above all the others and presented itself with horror and unspeakable force. It was my sacrilege of the Eucharist. An entire lifetime of injustice, violence, and impurity was eclipsed by the darkness of this offence against Jesus Christ. Indeed, I had exposed Him "to public shame" (Hebrews 6:6, GNB). During Mass in HMP Glenochil, Fr Andrew would permit some of us to hand out the body and blood of Jesus to other prisoners. I bitterly remembered handing out this sacred sacrament while totally stoned. I had mocked Jesus, and I was certain that this text was reminding me of it.

The words, "they are again crucifying the Son of God" spun round and round. The thought, *I am guilty of crucifying Jesus twice!... Crucifying Jesus twice... Crucifying Jesus twice!* would not leave me. I wanted to vomit. *Crucifying Jesus twice. How could such a thing be possible?* As I tried to clear my mind and reflect on this, I found myself looking directly at two condemning words within my solitary cell: *Double Cross* was boldly printed on the front of the gangster book I'd picked up earlier.

I'm damned, I thought. *I will not, I cannot be saved.*

I had "double crossed" my Saviour and could never be forgiven. The dread of this shook me to the core, and sweat formed as the foretaste of hell's anguish and the pangs of conscience assailed me. The stench of my life filled the cell, choking any hope. My sins appeared as an immovable mountain placed between God and me, and this dark mountain cast a cold shadow over my future.

God hates me. I was convinced. *He... He... He has rejected me.*

I broke down and began to weep – not just tears, but sobs, deep sobs from the very centre of my soul. That Jesus had died for me – for me – was brought home fully, and this was how I had lived in light of that knowledge. I wept uncontrollably and I didn't care who could hear my wailing among these tombs. I did not weep for my damnation, but for the Son of God, who was so beautiful. We did not deserve Him in this world.

I am a monster, an evil, wicked beast.

I wept for my Saviour's body – broken, His blood poured out – all of Himself, poured out because we needed it all; all of Him.

"HE'S SO GOOD, SO GOOD, SO GOOD, WHAT HAVE I DONE?" I cried, loudly and bitterly.

I had insulted and mocked the most beautiful expression of love in history – the death of Jesus remembered at the Mass. This sobbing went on and on. I could not keep myself from drowning in sorrow when I thought about the love of Jesus.

Then I found some words of Jesus that were addressed to hypocrites like me in His own day:

> *"Now then, you Pharisees clean the outside of*
> *your cup and plate, but inside you are full of*
> *violence and evil. Fools! Did not God, who made*
> *the outside, also make the inside? But give*
> *what is in your cups and plates to the poor, and*
> *everything will be ritually clean for you."*

Luke 11:39-41

Immediately, I pushed the alarm on my cell wall, and the screws came to the door. No sooner had they come, I began to take off my shoes. "Here," I said, "take these." I threw my shoes in front of them. "And all of my property, all the stuff in my cell back on the wing, please take it to reception; I'm going to hand it out at my next visit."

"Tony, what's wrong with you?" asked one of the screws.

"You're not going to do something daft, are you?" questioned another.

I could see in their faces that they thought I was about to do something drastic. Often a person about to commit suicide will hand his belongings out before doing the act. However, my reasons were different. As I had been "keeping out of trouble", which really meant no fights for about six months, I had managed to gain some privileges. My cell on the wing was packed with stuff; it was like Aladdin's cave in comparison to the cells of other convicts. My mates on the outside ensured I lacked nothing: I had a PlayStation and games, a DVD player, CDs, everything. I had ridiculously expensive clothing like Prada shoes and designer jeans. I had managed to stack up so much through staying out of fights, whereas in solitary you get nothing.

"All of it has to go," I insisted.

"Eh?" They looked at me, confused and concerned.

"Just take it to reception. It's all going to a charity shop."

They were bewildered. They took my stuff and a short while later they returned and handed me a pair of prison-issue shoes. They were horrible-looking things. The YOs used to call them "doutt flickers", because the type of person wearing them in prison was usually the guy who walked around the exercise yard picking up the used roll-ups (doutts) from the ground and smoking them – the con who could not afford any tobacco at the canteen. As well as the doutt flickers, I was given prison-issue jeans that were dyed so cheaply that the navy blue colouring would come off and stain my legs and shoes. I looked ridiculous, but didn't care in the slightest, as long as I no longer wore clothing that had been purchased through the pain of addicts.

Shortly after the screws left me, I was, for some unknown reason, reminded of Mrs Peterson, my primary school teacher. I recalled a day in her class when all of us children were sitting crossed-legged in front of her chair, and she began telling us that God was three-in-one and called "Trinity". She told us the story of St Patrick and how, when preaching to the pagans, he would use the shamrock to illustrate, in a limited way, the Trinity – three leaves but one stem; three persons but one God. All these years later, I could hear her telling me about the Father, the Son, and the Holy Spirit. In light of this, I determined to fast one day for each person of the Trinity. Though still utterly convinced that I was damned and that it was "impossible" for me to be forgiven, I nevertheless decided that this Jesus, this amazing person, still deserved to be followed. He had given everything for me and I had spat in His face. Even though I was going to hell, He was still worthy of being honoured and followed until the day I died.

I fasted one day for the Father, one day for the Son, and one day for the Holy Spirit, to say sorry to the Holy Trinity for all the evil I had done. Throughout those three days, the horrors of my sins were vividly presented and accompanied me through every second. They scorched my soul all the more painfully in light of Jesus' actions and the love He had shown by dying for me. A spotlight had been placed on my heart, and every stain could be easily seen. There was nowhere to hide from God's gaze. All my sins confronted me and stared me full in the face, filling me with the deepest shame and regret.

I felt completely shut out from the mercy of God. That God's friendship was lost remained my most bitter reflection. When I thought about this, I began to howl and groan from the very pit of my stomach. I had lost Jesus. I wailed and wept repeatedly throughout those three days. I had thought myself a tough guy before, a "go-ahead", up for anything and afraid of no one; I was nothing but a damned ruined fool. When I thought about my sacrilege of the Eucharist and disrespect in the fellowship meetings, I banged my head on the floor and attempted to rip my hair out, such was the despair at having insulted the Spirit of Grace. A terrible hopelessness enveloped me to such an extent that I felt as if I was already damned and numbered among the cursed. I wished I had never been born, and longed that the ground would swallow me up and drop me into everlasting nothingness. It was too much to bear. I had fallen from the hand of love itself and was brutally conscious of it. I wanted to cry out, "Let the mountains fall on me and the hills cover me" (see Luke 23:30). That would be easier than receiving the just wrath of God.

After this three-day period of fasting and prayer, I was worn out completely. There had been little let-up for sleep – no rest or relief, and I was exhausted. On the fourth day I didn't throw my food down the toilet; I ate it and I could feel it giving me energy again.

While reflecting on this decision to follow Jesus fully, out of nowhere came a horrible cloud of darkness. *What are you doing?* it mocked. *Are you going to let people see you like this? Look at the state of you!*

I looked at my shoes and felt a pang of embarrassment in my stomach. My jeans were a disgrace too.

You're going to be laughed at big time – look at you. You're turning into one of these pure dafties. What next – a sandwich board and a megaphone? Do you hear them laughing at you? the voice mocked. I had just told several cons who had heard my crying from under the steel doors that I was going to walk after Jesus for the rest of my life. I could hear faint murmuring and laughter. Still this darkness continued: *You're a joke.*

These horrible thoughts emanated emptiness and carried the same sense of forsakenness I had experienced as child. *THERE IS NO GOD. These Christians only believe what they want to believe. It's a crutch.*

It was relentless…

Where is He then? Your head's fried, spent far too long in the Seg! Fifteen months' solitary will fry your head.

My fingers tightened and my knuckles became white as I clenched my fists.

All these "signs" are circular beliefs. TONY, GET A GRIP OF YOURSELF, MAN, give yourself a shake. You actually want to believe in God so much that your mind is constructing all these "coincidences" in a way to make you believe them. You're seeing and hearing what you want to!

Had I snapped? I looked in the mirror: I had a swollen face from having spent days crying. Large bags hung under my eyes from no sleep. Even the screws were thinking I was losing it, and clearly, so did the cons. I felt awful and looked disgraceful.

Everything was thrown into doubt – all of it. From Fr

John coming to see me six months earlier and telling me about the song that changed his life, to me going back to my cell and turning my radio on and hearing it. From my going to take another man's life, then right before I stabbed him, my friend's wounds making him appear so much like Jesus that it stopped me killing. Not to mention God getting someone to sing out the very words I was reading in the Bible, exactly as I was reading, "Come back to me." Even the smaller coincidence of the book *Double Cross*, when I couldn't stop thinking about crucifying Jesus twice. All of this was thrown into the air by these dark thoughts that assailed me, tossing me into confusion.

I just needed a sign, something to show me that all that had happened wasn't just a crazed construction in the mind of a man. I walked over to my cell window and looked through the bars, right up to the sky. "God," I whispered, "if I saw a dove right now, I would really believe." I prayed this prayer in earnest, remembering, in the far reaches of my memory, reading or hearing about the dove being a symbol of the Holy Spirit. I wasn't trying to test or bargain with God. I had made up my mind to follow His Son, but now I was racked with an interior pain caused by the dark doubts that unceasingly invaded my mind.

You fool. You're going to give your entire life over to something you can't be sure is true – dafty!

Nevertheless, I stood there looking earnestly out of the cell window for God to send a dove; then all these doubts would have to go. I waited, looking expectantly for a miracle. After everything that had happened, I was more than prepared to ask for it. I stood there, staring out of that window like a fool. I waited there for about

147

ten minutes, and it felt like an age. Nothing. Not one bird, not even one of the squawking, screeching prison gulls that were always hanging around. I turned around, absolutely gutted. I could feel the next volley of doubts readying themselves to bombard me. Then, glancing over to my bed, I noticed that the book on animals was open, and there, staring right at me, was a picture of a collared dove!

I laughed loudly, then fell on my knees. Let the demons say it was another coincidence. My God had answered my prayer, even mine! *Could there be mercy for me?* I was certain I was damned, that God had abandoned me like I deserved, that He couldn't be interested in me, but He had answered my prayer. My prayer! I started to cry. He had answered my prayer – even mine. I had abandoned hope, since what hope was there for someone like me? I had outraged God; I was an animal – an animal. I had hurt people, done shameful and treacherous things – why would He answer me?

Just then, as I was thanking God and weeping, I was filled up – filled with a supernatural peace. I could feel the love of God as it poured into my heart. I could actually feel it! I could feel it, and with it came the most unspeakable joy! Oh what a joy: I laughed, I cried, I sang. I had peace, an unshakable peace, a peace like I had never known. I was in a maximum security prison, inside a solitary cell, and I was freer than I had ever been in my life!

The peace of God, which surpasses all understanding, will guard your hearts and your minds in Christ Jesus.

Philippians 4:7

This peace also surpasses all *mis*understanding, because even if I wanted to doubt God, I could not. An undeniable *power* had entered my life, and with it a great confidence and trust in the mercy of God. Those dark doubts could no longer touch me. I was free – so free. I thought I was cursed and cut off from God, but where I deserved death, He had given me life, and where there is life there is hope.

> *For you shall go out in joy*
> *and be led forth in peace;*
> *the mountains and the hills before you*
> *shall break forth into singing,*
> *and all the trees of the field shall clap their*
> *hands.*

Isaiah 55:12

I walked over to the cell window and was staggered at what I saw: everything looked so beautiful.

A veil had been removed from my eyes, and for the first time I could see. It seemed as if I had been experiencing life through an old transistor radio; now everything was in high definition – sharp, colourful, and incredibly beautiful. Creation was a celebration praising God; everything pulsed with the life of God and spoke "God". All things were proclaiming His greatness, His kindness, His mercy. Even the little bugs running across the outside of my window revealed more of His goodness. My world had been rocked; I would never be the same again, I truly was "born of God" (John 1:13).

11

You Shall Receive Power

HMP Glenochil

The unspeakable joy! I did not think such happiness existed or was even possible. I was walking around my cell, now singing, now laughing.

"Right, Gielty, you're going back up to the wing," an officer informed me after opening the cell door. "We'll get you taken back up after shift change this evening," said another. "Do you want to use the phone in the meantime?"

Before I could respond, he cut in again, saying, "Oh, and by the way, your mate is okay. He got out to hospital in time."

When I heard this I wanted to leap for joy: this news truly completed my delight.

I was just so filled up with love, a supernatural love which seemed to want to burst out of me. During the phone call home, when my twin brother Michael answered the family phone, I couldn't stop telling him, again and again, that I loved him.

"Are you alright?" he asked.

"I love you, Michael. I just want to tell you that." I was unable to contain myself.

He was really confused now.

"Is Ma or Da in?" I asked.

"No," he replied.

"Tell them I called and that I really, really love them," I told him.

This was obviously too much for Michael: "You've cracked!"

"Cheers, Michael. I'll call you later," I said cheerily. "Oh, and I love you, bro."

"What the…?"

I returned to my cell and began stripping my bedding in preparation for the move back up to the wing, a wing full of hundreds of Scotland's criminals. Suddenly, out of nowhere, dark thoughts returned.

Are you really going to let them see you like this? Look at the state of you.

I looked down at my shoes and at the rest of my clothing. I was getting ready to step back onto a wing filled with hundreds of prisoners and I looked like a madman. Embarrassment and fear were set to enter my heart. I refused to let them take hold and stopped them. I focused on the joy of being forgiven and knowing it. *Oh, the assurance of sins blotted out!* I was now forgiven, all my sins and crimes taken away. All of them! I determined to proclaim it; I would speak it to everyone I knew, and through this little renunciation of even the clothing stained with sin (Jude 1:23), I would be able to do so in a manner that would challenge things many cons set store by. Drugs, money, clothing, and status: I had renounced them all, and because I knew there was such a power watching over me, I had confidence. Though I knew that many would consider me a weirdo as externally I looked so shabby, internally I felt keenly the power of the living God.

Patricia, who had heard about all that had happened, came to see me just before I left the solitary wing.

"I knew you would come," I said, smiling.

I could see that Patricia had not known what to think or expect. The simple facts pointed to me being in some way involved with the stabbing.

"How are you?" she asked. There was no judgment, no condemnation, just concern.

"Patricia, God has... God has..."

I broke down, weeping. I tried to explain to her about Amos, the books, the power of the Holy Spirit, and found it impossible because of the tears. They streamed involuntarily down my face as I considered how much God had forgiven me. I felt so unworthy and yet so loved at the same time; it was too much for my soul to bear.

Please take my life, God. I am unworthy. Please take me; if you leave me I'll still sin, I prayed inwardly. I had become so afraid of offending this God any more, He was just so good.

I could not communicate the joy and the love I was experiencing in my soul, but Patricia smiled reassuringly. Regaining enough control of my speech, I was able to offer her a single word: "Wonderful." I kept repeating this word until I was finally able to gain enough composure to explain what had happened and my current state of being. "Wonderful," I told her. "God has done something wonderful to me."

I found it impossible to articulate all that was going on in my soul. Patricia just smiled and said reassuringly, "This is what I have been telling you is possible with God."

After I had spent some time with Patricia, the officers came to take me back to the hall. I could feel something powerful at work in me, which was causing me to love – everything and everyone. I found I could no longer bear any negative thought toward anyone without feeling it unjustified and without finding something positive to say. In the past, I had fed on negativity and had been immersed in bitter criticism of both myself and others. Even the prison officers, whom I had formerly passionately hated and had taken pleasure in hating, were among those for whom it took some effort on my part to stop myself from hugging. *What on earth was going on with me?* As we left the segregation unit, I knew for certain that this time would be the last time. Love had violently taken possession of me.

As soon as I returned to my cell, I began taking down the posters of women that were on the wall, and getting rid of everything that I understood to be displeasing to God. As I systematically worked my way round my cell, bagging up the possessions I felt were no longer acceptable, I was overflowing with joy and serenity. I felt so alive and full of peace, joy, and love.

Then suddenly, without warning, what can only be described as an oppressive, unseen presence entered the cell, instantly identifiable by the smell of burning that accompanied it. I froze with terror. I believed in hell, yet only in some far-off "day-you-died" sense, and even then I had shifted between believing in a place of annihilation and a temporal state of being on earth, as when people talk about a "living hell". Yet now it was like hell itself was reaching up and breaking into my cell. Out of nowhere I was being presented with a sharp sensory experience of that place – or at least, something from that place. The smell was unnatural, as though the scent itself carried pain. Scorched and suffocating, it filled me with a horrid hopelessness. I wanted to cry for help, but I clenched my fists and whispered, "Oh God, oh my God."

By now it was late into the night. I had been up sifting through what was left of my belongings. I kept whispering after Jesus, knowing that most of the prison wing outside my door was asleep. "Oh Jesus, my Jesus, help me," I appealed. My mind became full of horrible blasphemies related to God, His holy mother and the saints. The thoughts were relentless and bombarded me for hours, forcing me to lie down on the bed, trembling and sweating. *If these mental assaults don't stop soon, I'll lose my mind,* I thought, wondering why God was permitting this. I was thoroughly terrified, even though there was no physical form or corporeal presence to see. My mind was under intense pressure, as if at any moment it would fold into an abyss...

***

I awoke on my bed in my cell the next day, exhausted and relieved to discover that the thoughts, blasphemies, and suffocating scent were gone. *But why had God allowed this?* Although my joy had been eclipsed the night before, it now continued with me as strong as ever. This awful experience was a reminder of all I was being saved from, as well as the reality of the enemy.

For we do not wrestle against flesh and blood,
but against the rulers, against the authorities,
against the cosmic powers over this present
darkness, against the spiritual forces of evil
in the heavenly places. Therefore take up the
whole armour of God, that you may be able to
withstand in the evil day, and having done all, to
stand firm.

Ephesians 6:12-13

Furthermore, that smell would henceforth herald the approach of other demons and announce their presence clearly and distinctly.

After the morning count, when the screws came and opened the cell door, I rushed over and closed it again. I needed a moment: after all, I would be walking out to see hundreds of men who had known me as a "go-ahead", someone they respected and even feared. Once again, I glanced down at my feet to see the awful prison issue shoes and clothing. *What were the guys going to say when they found out I had not only given my clothes away, but had also got rid of my mobile phone?*

I strengthened myself with the verse, "Looking to Jesus, the founder and perfecter of our faith, who for the joy that was set before him endured the cross, despising the shame, and is seated at the right hand of the throne of God" (Hebrews 12:2). Recalling the example of St Louis, I was ashamed at my hesitation, for he had entered St Sulpice and attended the Sorbonne University after having swapped his clothes with a beggar. "Oh God," I whispered. "Give me the grace to despise this shame." I then walked out onto the wing.

It seemed like the eyes of the whole wing were upon me. They hadn't seen me since the stabbing and I knew many would be eager to speak with me about what had happened, as well as investigate what revenge I was planning. They looked at me in astonishment. It was breakfast time, usually a time when sleepy cons drag their knuckles along the floor as they yawn, scratch, and prepare for another day in jail. Not this morning. Many looked at me with a sharp awareness; others in a puzzled manner. As I collected my breakfast cereal and sat down, the atmosphere became more difficult, with the silence only broken by the occasional snigger.

"What happened to you, Tony?" asked Steve, a genuinely concerned con sitting at my table.

"What do you mean?" I asked, lifting a milky spoon of cheap rice crispies into my mouth and crunching away as if nothing was out of the ordinary.

"I mean, well…" he then exploded, swearing in pure frustration, no longer able to contain himself. Another guy, Peter, interjected, "Come on, Tony, what the…?"

"Listen, lads," I said abruptly, not wanting them to go any further with the swearing or the confused questioning. By this time, others were gathering round the table. "I have given my life to Jesus so I've given all my things that were gained illegally to charity."

"Everything?" asked Justin, probing cautiously, trying to discover if the phone was also gone.

"Everything!"

"You're kidding!" he said, spraying the table with milk and cereal as he spoke. "I know what you're up to, ha ha…" he laughed, walking off. I could see by his sly smile he was thinking this was all a front.

"What?" Martin continued in disbelief. "You've got rid

of your dooda?" "Dooda" was a reference to the phone.

"Of course!" I replied.

"Are you mental?" he questioned, staring me straight in the eyes, assessing my mental health. He knew that by getting rid of my phone, I was also getting rid of the ability to smuggle things into the prison through unmonitored calls. This was a devastating blow to the lads, since they looked to me as their source.

"I have to go God's way now, mate," I told him firmly.

"Yeah, but even God would shake His head at that one," said Stevie, who shared a cell with Martin. "And as for giving your Prada shoes away, well, you're definitely going to hell for that!"

I just smiled. They were simply trying to make light of what for them was a crazy situation. After all, just the week before I had been one of the boys, smoking weed and organizing pick-ups and drop-offs. I had been attending services and had demonstrated religious leanings, but that, in their eyes, was acceptable. However, seeing me like this shocked them. They were so puzzled. They continued firing questions at me, trying desperately to stay calm and not have someone overhear them. As they spoke, others came over. It became a hustle of cons not so much coming to speak to me but to stare, as if at a dead man during a wake. Usually each camp has its own table, a piece of steel furniture bolted to the ground with half a dozen seats also strategically bolted into the ground around it. But today everyone was gathering around just one table.

My attention was drawn to the light through the bars at the end of the wing that I could see over some shoulders. I could see a blue sky, contrasted beautifully with creamy clouds, all of which seemed to be continually speaking "God". Everything now spoke "God". Hardened faces, wearied with internal struggles, also spoke "God". I was looking at people and creation as if for the very first time, and it all shouted "GOD".

This tranquil awareness was agitated only by the swearing I was picking up from the conversations around the table. Swearing had never bothered me before, but it suddenly became grating to hear, particularly when blasphemies were added. Inwardly it grieved me. This, too, was a new and surreal experience.

"Tony?" came a voice, interrupting my thoughts. "He's daydreaming."

"I can hear you," I said, then I recalled the last words I had heard. Stevie had just joked about going to hell, and I shuddered as I remembered the previous night and the smell of hell in my cell. I got up and left the table.

"Where you going, man?" asked Stevie, who was right in the middle of saying something to me. I had an overwhelming need to go and pray. I wanted to break down crying for these men who knew nothing of the gospel, nothing of heaven and nothing of hell. He had only used the word jokingly, but I could not bear to hear that word. "Hell" was now too real. I rushed into my cell and closed the door before anyone could see the tears.

What is happening to me? Get it together, man.

***

The friends who had once been part of my camp now slowly but steadily began to distance themselves from me. This was fine, because it was getting tougher and tougher to be around them as they planned their heists and described their conquests. It was also interesting to watch those who would have feared me become bolder around me, as if my decision to turn to Christ made me weak. So I would often hear names like "John the Baptist" and "Moses".

I continued to read about the lives of the saints. I noticed how they were consumed with a love of God and a love for their neighbours, and how this love of neighbour was inextricably linked with a tireless effort to work for the salvation of other souls. As I continued to read Scripture, I could clearly understand texts such as, "And there is salvation in no one else, for there is no other name under heaven given among men by which we must be saved" (Acts 4:12); "For there is one God, and there is one mediator between God and men, the man Christ Jesus" (1 Timothy 2:5); "Jesus said to him, 'I am the way, and the truth, and the life. No one comes to the Father except through me" (John 14:6).

This burdened me deeply for the men who surrounded me. I felt I was in the very place where Satan was enthroned, in the dark ambitions and agendas of the criminals around me. But in this place of darkness the light would shine even brighter, and the darkness could not bring it down. I felt strongly that God was at hand, and the sacred heart of Jesus was passionately on fire for these sinners just like me.

"He's had the heart ripped clean out of him," said one lifer, playing pool with other prisoners while keenly discussing why I was no longer involved in the gang scene. Instantly, my old nature reacted. *Look at him,* I thought, and I stared straight at him. *Walk over there and smash him,* my thoughts demanded. *Take him into the cell and let him know you're not an idiot: you could break him up with a couple of punches.* Though God had begun a work in me, the old nature and its pride was strong. Anger began to rise.

No! I inwardly renounced these thoughts, and immediately I discerned the scorched, suffocating smell. My heart was moved with pity for this man, even though he was insulting me. He was so blind to the reality of spiritual things, and this was all he had known.

"I have not lost my heart, Davy. I've found it," I said gently, with no hint of annoyance or sarcasm. I replied to him as I would a friend. His face went red and I could see he was embarrassed and a little saddened at what he had said to me. Later he came and apologized.

There were countless scenarios like this in the jail, where the demons would try to stir up the flesh for a reaction, but the smell of burning often unmasked their attempts and made me all the more determined to reach my fellow prisoners with the love of Jesus.

I became increasingly lonely, as I found I didn't have much in common with anyone inside any more. I just could not stomach listening to jail chat. It became agonizing to have to listen to trivial talk, and all I wanted to discuss were eternal things. I felt so frustrated. I longed to be able to tear back the veil and show them the things of God.

As a kid I had been filled with despair at the fate of humanity heading for the grave, especially as I observed people going about their lives as if nothing was wrong. Even then, the thought of death had been too much, and it was this that ultimately had sent me on a path of destruction. But now, as I reflected on the eternal torment of a place for people without Christ, it broke my heart. I prayed earnestly about this and said my Rosary every day. No matter how difficult things became in prison, the Rosary always brought peace and prevented me from despairing. I felt I had a weapon, even in prison, through which I could pray for awakening in other souls. It did not disappoint: time after time, the Holy Rosary of the Blessed Virgin brought about a spiritual awareness for the most hardened of prisoners in the most unlikely of circumstances. "For the weapons of our warfare are not of the flesh but have divine power to destroy strongholds" (2 Corinthians 10:4).

***

"That's it. I'm going to smash his skull!" shouted Ecky, rushing into my cell, panting and out of breath.

"Calm down," I said. "Take a seat and tell me what's wrong."

"My new co-pilot is a devil worshipper. Man, can you believe it, a devil worshipper? A fully fledged devil worshipper, man," Ecky said, panting and looking up at the cell's ceiling, as if staring into the heavens and asking why.

"What, like a satanist?" I asked.

"I'm going to smash him," Ecky said, seething.

"Ecky, get it together, man. Tell me what's happened."

"I'll tell you alright," he said. "So you know how I was getting a new cellmate?"

"Yeah."

"Well, he comes swaggering right in – doesn't even introduce himself – sticks a wooden plaque with 'satan' written on it above my door and starts giving me heavy attitude. Then he finds out I'm a Christian and man, well... I just... just... I'm going to kill him, man!"

Eck was from the travelling community, and I had come to know him very well after hearing him share his story one evening at the prison fellowship meeting. He had known crime all his days and, always knowing how to turn his hand to make a quick buck, he soon became deeply involved in criminal syndicates. So zealous was his pursuit of money that, after one significant robbery, he described pouring the money out on his caravan floor and throwing it in the air shouting, "THIS IS MY GOD! THIS IS MY GOD!"

Not long after that, he lost his firstborn son. This brought his world crashing down. It was a double blow as twelve days earlier he had lost his father. In his testimony, Ecky described how he had woken up after his father's funeral to find his child dead. When Eck told this story, he admitted that he struggled to read the passage from the Gospel that says, "A voice is heard in Ramah, weeping and loud lamentation, Rachel weeping for her children; she refused to be comforted, because they are no more" (Matthew 2:18), as it reminded him of the terrible wail that had gone up for their child that morning.

Eck stated that he had gone from bad to worse; his life became a trail of destruction, like a man who had lost everything and cared about nothing. Then Eck's wife Kathleen became pregnant with another child. However, there were significant complications with the pregnancy, and their little boy, Reece, was born at twenty-four weeks, "on the cusp of viability" according to the doctor. He weighed only 1lb 7oz and had no hair, eyebrows, or finger nails. He was a tiny bundle clothed in transparent skin. Yet Ecky did not see this tiny, vulnerable life as anything other than his son, his baby boy, who was now on the verge of death. Then the medics informed Eck and Kathleen that their son had contracted MRSA and one of his lungs had collapsed. The medics broke the news to both of them that they were going to lose their child. Hearing this news, and desperately determined not to lose a second son, Eck turned to God as his last hope, and sent for the minister.

In his testimony, Ecky described the tremendous peace that the minister brought as he entered the place where little Reece lay fighting for his life, with all the family gathered round. The minister calmly placed his hands on the incubator and prayed. Before leaving them, he turned and said to them assuredly, "He will make it."

Astonishingly, the medics noticed a significant difference on the machines and computers around the incubator. The machine that was reading the level of oxygen circulating the body was now reading at 100 per cent. Eck also noticed that the nurse turned the amount of oxygen down to the same level as everyone breathes. Later they found that the MRSA was gone, and that the scarring in Reece's lungs was also gone.

In consequence of this enormous miracle which had taken place in the tiny body of his son, Eck became a passionate Christian. Following his decision to follow for Christ, Ecky had to face up to his previous lifestyle as a criminal and, for crimes he had committed before he was Christian, he had been sent into prison. Yet the providence of God had now brought us together on the same wing and made us good friends. Although I was saddened to watch my brother separated from his young family, I was so thankful that he was now beside me in Glenochil, since prison can be a lonely place for a disciple.

Eck's father had raised him never to back down and always to stand up for himself. Now, with the arrival of this confrontational co-pilot, he was being challenged to abide by the code of love given by his heavenly Father. This code was being tested to the very limits: he had no choice about who he lived with. It was hard enough for guys like us to leave criminal pasts, to have to learn to walk away from a fight within a culture where standing your ground meant everything, but the added torment of having the faith that had saved him and his child undermined and attacked appeared too much for Eck.

I decided to go over and meet Ecky's new co-pilot to see what could be done.

"Hi, my name's Anthony," I said, stretching out my hand.

The guy was a young red-haired man called Andy, and he had what we cons called "the forty-yard stare" – eyes that seemed to look at you as if you were far away, the kind of eyes found in psychiatric wards.

"One of that mob are you? A total Jesus freak as well?" he asked, mockingly.

"Yes," I said without hesitation. "I love Jesus." The look he gave me showed his contempt and that his suspicions were confirmed. "Anyway," I continued, "my cell's just over the landing if you need anything. Since you've just arrived, feel free to come by and I'll help you out with anything you're short of. I've got plenty of tea and coffee you can borrow until your canteen comes."

I then headed back to my cell where Ecky was waiting. "Eck," I said, "just give it another day."

"Man, I'm not sure I can," he replied.

"You can, bro. Look to Jesus."

After Ecky left, I began to pray the Rosary for Andy. As I knelt down I resolved not to get up until I had said all of the Rosary for him. During these intercessions, I felt the deep internal witness of the Spirit. That night, comforted by the Comforter, I went to bed.

The following morning, after my devotions, there

was a rap on my cell door. Without waiting for a reply, Andy walked straight in without a word. He was pale and trembling. "Can I speak with you?" he asked. His pallid face and shaking hands made him look terrible.

He began to describe what had happened. During the night, he had had a disturbing dream. "This is going to sound mental, man, but I'm just going to say as it is."

"Go ahead," I said gently.

"I... I... saw him. P-p-p-pure evil, man," he stuttered and began to shake. As I got up to make him a cup of tea in the cell, I knew straight away of whom he was speaking. He became more inaudible as he continued whispering, "Evil. Pure, pure evil." He could not stop repeating these words. He was a grown man, powerfully built, yet he had been reduced to a quivering wreck.

Then suddenly he stopped his muttering and looked up at me, piercing me with his eyes. "I heard you," he said.

"What do you mean?" I asked.

"I could hear you praying for me throughout my dream last night."

I was shocked. Nobody knew I had been praying for him. I had been alone in my cell.

"That's astonishing," I said. "I was praying for you. I asked the Blessed Virgin to intercede for you."

Staring at the floor, he said, "I know. In my dream I could see him, and all the time I could see his hatred for me and for God; his absolute evil hatred. I can't describe it, man; horrible, man, pure horrible, Anthony. Within the dream I could feel the voice of God saying to the devil, 'We have chained you.' I know this is to stop him carrying out all the evil he desires. I... I..." he began to stutter again "I... I had always felt respect for the devil, but Anthony," he looked up at me, and once more his eyes pierced me as he stared straight at me, "there is no such thing as reason or room for discussion – he is hate."

He quickly placed the cup on the floor, spilling some in the process, and covered his face with his hands. I heard the muffled groans as he continued saying, "His eyes, his eyes; O God, his eyes." He trembled as he remembered seeing Satan looking at him, seeing in his gaze the depth of the enemy's hatred and pride. Then he spoke in such a way as to leave me in no doubt that this dream was of God. Here was a man who had never read a Bible, who knew nothing of the things of God, and yet he proceeded to tell me, "We are charged to share with everyone the message of Jesus, in His name... in His..." he broke off, unable to finish his sentence.

After regaining enough composure, he turned to me and said, "You know, every time I mentioned the name of Jesus in my dream, Satan backed further away from me. He could not bear that name." I could see that God had revealed Himself powerfully to Andy.

***

There were so many occasions when I saw God working through the power of the Rosary. On another day, I decided to pray for a Muslim man with whom I had become good friends. After praying for him one evening, I was assured the Holy Spirit would move. The following day he ran down the route filled with prisoners returning from their respective work groups and grabbed me by the arm. "Last night I dreamt I was walking on the wrong side of the road, when out of the horizon a car with its headlights on came speeding toward me. I couldn't move, then right before it smashed into me, I screamed, 'JESUS!' Then suddenly I was on the other side of the road, safe and sound. What does this mean?"

Through the use of the Rosary, I found that the more I prayed for people, the less convincing I had to do. God went before me, and He was far better at convincing people than I was.

***

After many months, lots of prisoners continued to see me as a weirdo, but many would also come to my cell and we would pray. Often hardened cons on my wing would make their way round just to ask me to say a prayer for their families. At times, Muslim inmates would harass me in the exercise yard, where they could be seen, but then would come back when they could not be seen and ask questions about Christ. They would ask me to pray for them when their mother was sick or a family member was in trouble. Many of them were of mixed race or Afro-Caribbean origins and had turned to Islam within the prison system as the alternative to what they perceived was a "white way".

In the six months before the attack on Matt and my subsequent deep experience of God's love, I had been reading Scripture daily, but afterwards I began to devour it. Somewhere in the readings that Patricia was still giving me, I read these words of St Jerome: "Ignorance of scripture is ignorance of Christ." I took this statement to heart and read the whole Bible again and again.

An immense desire to learn new things began to awaken in me, and with the awakening of my soul to God came a divine flavour to every endeavour because, now that I had something to live for, I determined to do it with all my heart. I wanted to use the remainder of my time in prison to learn. I was not ashamed to begin elementary courses in maths and English. I did not know how to type, let alone work a computer, so I signed up for IT lessons. I was twenty years old in 2006 and completely computer illiterate. I remember the teacher's reaction after she instructed me to do a short essay on anything I liked – her concern when she noticed me writing "SA" instead of "essay".

I signed up for so many courses within the education department that they allowed me to do full-time education, which meant that all my mornings and afternoons would be taken up with classes. I became so excited about it after I read in Proverbs:

> *My son, if you receive my words*
> *and treasure up my commandments with you,*
> *making your ear attentive to wisdom*
> *and inclining your heart to understanding;*
> *yes, if you call out for insight*
> *and raise your voice for understanding,*
> *if you seek it like silver*
> *and search for it as for hidden treasures,*
> *then you will understand the fear of the Lord*
> *and find the knowledge of God.*

Proverbs 2:1–5

I sought to apply this as literally as I could by asking for as much education as was possible. By 2007 I had completed a Scottish Group Award in Software Development and Information Systems, as well as achieved a Higher in Communication. Soon after this, the education department in HMP Glenochil allowed me to start helping other prisoners from different areas of the prison learn to read and write. This gave me access to many of the different wings to meet and speak privately with other prisoners and so tell them about Jesus.

I volunteered to be a "Prison Listener" which, as the name suggests, meant listening to prisoners. The Listeners were trained by the Samaritans in preparation for listening to the suicidal and self-harming, and those who just needed someone to talk to. We could be called upon day or night and were bound by the strictest confidentiality. We were available for the prisoners who needed a fellow con, someone they felt could truly understand them. This, too, opened up many opportunities to pray with people and share Jesus with them.

After being informed that I was to begin teaching a fellow prisoner in a separate wing basic reading and writing skills, I made my way to his cell. A small, sturdy man in his late forties with rounded shoulders, deep eyes, bushy, greying hair, and a moustache met me at the door.

"Hello," he said, welcoming me in.

"Hi," I replied.

"Are you a Christian?" he asked immediately.

"Yes, I am. How could you tell?" I asked, curious at his question.

"It's easy to spot a Christian," he replied.

Interested to find out where his line of questioning was coming from, I asked, "Are you Christian?"

"Yes," he replied firmly.

He put the kettle on and we began sharing some tea and telling each other our testimonies. Willie wept as he told me that he was serving time for causing an accident while under the influence. In prison he had rededicated his life to Christ.

Willie asked me, "Do you want to pray together?"

"Yes," I replied. I had already been built up so much through hearing his testimony. As he prayed, the tremendous power of the Holy Spirit filled the cell and filled us both with such joy that we began to laugh. I called upon God for more, and Willie responded, "If you want more, give out more." I looked at him: his face was radiant and glowing under the Holy Spirit.

"Your face," I said. "It's shining."

"I know, brother," he replied. "If you want to experience more, begin inviting people for prayer in Jesus' name!"

I was just visiting Willie and was in another wing where I didn't know anyone. Despite the power and joy we were experiencing, my reservations began to mount. Nevertheless, the joy and the thought that more could be added made me open Willie's cell door. Immediately, the people outside unconsciously began coming toward the cell, as if pulled along by some supernatural magnet. Prisoners began to congregate outside the cell, and as they continued their conversations they didn't seem to notice that they were all hanging around closely in the one area.

"Do you want to come for some prayer?" I asked one of the men outside.

"Eh?" he replied, quite surprised. "No."

He looked embarrassed and moved away, as did the others. But despite their resistance, and my reluctance, I found the more I overcame myself and stepped out to reach others, the more of God's presence and power I experienced.

As I said goodbye to Willie and headed back to my own wing, I was both overjoyed and perplexed. I had gone along to teach another prisoner to read and write, and he had ended up teaching me so much about God. Every other day I began to meet with prisoners in my cell to read the word of God and pray – the consolations and power of the Holy Spirit were unspeakable. And around this time I began speaking in tongues. I was unable to find release or expression except in tongues. It came naturally to me and always left my soul with clarity and peace. However, I found that the only prisoners who would commit to coming for prayer were the most broken and unpopular prisoners: the rejected, the loners, the socially awkward, and the cons with learning difficulties. Yet it was these "little ones" who became the witnesses of wonderful answers to prayer. God was truly present among us, but even in prison it was hidden from the proud and revealed to the children (Luke 10:21).

I had many talks with other prisoners, and I would hear stories of what they had witnessed. One night, as a Listener, I was called to the suicide cell, where I met with a lad called Matthew. He was about twenty-three years old and his face was terribly scarred, with burn marks all over his face and down his neck. His appearance was frightful to look at, yet he welcomed me in, lay down on the bed, and began telling me about how he had gotten his burns and how he had almost died. I just listened.

"After getting drunk one night I drank some petrol and lit it. I went to a place so awful; terror overwhelmed me. There was master over us and it was terrible; it was terrible," he said, lost in the horror of what he had witnessed. Then, as if coming to, he said sharply, "Leave now. I'm tired."

"What did you see when you died?" I asked, unwilling to leave him in this state.

"I cannot go back there; it was awful," he said. "Time for you to leave."

I never saw this man again.

***

I became terribly burdened to share this message of the gospel. I felt personally responsible for witnessing to everyone I met, and felt keenly the words of Paul: "Woe to me if I do not preach the gospel!" (1 Corinthians 9:16). I therefore made the most of every opportunity. I was convinced of no higher calling, no higher ideal, than to live for Jesus who had given everything for us. Nothing was of more importance than telling men how they could be saved from a lost eternity.

12

May They Be One?

HMP Glenochil

Sick of my frequent recourse to the intercession of the
Blessed Virgin in my prayers, and also my request for the
intercession of the saints, a few of the more passionate
evangelical Christian prisoners at prayer meetings began
to challenge me on this. One day down in the library,
where we went for the chess club, John, a fellow brother,
was the first to take me up.

"Anthony, where in the Bible does it tell us to pray to
saints?" he asked.

"You ask that as if the saints are somehow the end
in themselves, but as Catholics we ask saints to pray for
us, just like we ask our brothers and sisters to pray for us
here."

"Where in the Bible does it say we can speak with the
dead?"

I was surprised he was challenging me in front of the
other cons, who were nodding in agreement with him.

"Mark 9:4 clearly describes Jesus in prayer discussing things with Moses and Elijah, two Old Testament saints, and although Elijah had not died, Moses had. Both had left this world, and their presence on the mountain with Jesus is an indicator that we can be helped on our earthly mission, just as Jesus was by those who had gone before Him. After all, isn't Jesus Christ our pattern?"

And so it started. The use of icons was next, with the statues and crucifixes, which broadened out into a discussion on tradition, and whether or not only those things which could be clearly proved by Scripture were to be followed. I was very hurt, both by what was said and the way it was said. We moved on to who was responsible for the Bible that John and those backing him up were referring to...

"We just believe in the Bible," said Rab.

"I love the Bible. Don't make out I am being unfaithful to God's word," I replied.

"You are," said Fraser.

"Who do you think decided the canon?" I asked.

"Eh?" asked John, looking perplexed. "What do you mean, canon?"

"The canon of Scripture," I said exasperatedly "The Bible. Who decided what books should be in it?"

"The Bible is the word of God," said Fraser, quite satisfied with his response.

"Yes, but why do we have what we have in it?"

"Because God said what should be in it."

"And who did He tell?"

"The born-again believers" replied Fraser.

"Exactly: the church. It was the eyewitnesses who handed down the Holy Tradition, which includes the accounts of Jesus as well the New Testament letters. The church preserves in full all that has been entrusted to her, including sacred Scripture and issues concerning worship – and that's what we call tradition."

"But Jesus condemned the Pharisees for their 'traditions' that He said nullify the word of God," answered John.

"I'm not talking about man-made traditions, like those of the Pharisees; I'm talking about the God-given Tradition."

"Where in the Bible does it talk about that?" asked Fraser.

"Fraser, do yourself a favour and read 2 Thessalonians 2:15."

He grabbed his Bible and began flicking through the New Testament searching for 2 Thessalonians. I could see that he loved the Bible. It was evident by the many pages that were full of illuminated highlights and underscored verses. He read aloud, " 'So then, brothers, stand firm and hold to the traditions that you were taught by us, either by our spoken word or by our letter.' So what?"

"There is an oral as well as a written tradition handed down to us. It says, 'by our spoken word or letter'. This is what the Catholic Church keeps, and this is also the word of God."

"The Bible is the only authority, the ground of truth concerning the faith," proclaimed John, still looking over at the others for approval.

"Yes, John, but the Bible itself states that the church is 'a pillar and buttress of the truth', in 1 Timothy 3:15."

"Dodgy doctrines and dead religion," concluded Fraser, really not willing to listen.

I was very hurt by this. Fraser had recently spent a long time within a passionate evangelical setting being discipled and learning Bible verses and Christian principles in order to remain free from a life of addiction. We had become really good friends, meeting to read the word and pray together, and my Catholicism had not been an issue before now. John was from another wing. He had a big personality and was really respected by other cons. So he was a real support for us coming together for worship in the prison. Rab, on the other hand, cared more about truth and enjoyed debate, but it was apparent that they all were getting tired of my Catholic tendencies in the meetings, and felt the need to challenge me.

"Come on, Anthony, what about Mary?" asked Fraser. "The Catholic Church puts her on a higher pedestal than Jesus."

"Jesus Christ is God, and the whole church recognizes that in comparison to Him, she is nothing, since He alone is," I replied, getting a bit weary. "God never did have need of her and never has need of anyone since He has only to will and it is." I was paraphrasing St Louis de Montfort's teaching here, but it didn't win the argument.

"So what's all the fuss about her, then?" asked Fraser.

"If by fuss you mean honour, then she is worthy of honour because although He did not have to, God *did* choose to make use of her in His plan for saving humanity, making her the mother of God."

"God doesn't have a mother; He's eternal. That's heresy," said John.

"What's heresy?" asked Rab.

"Heresy is wrong belief," I informed Rab.

"Actually, John, you'll find that not to call Mary the Mother of God is heresy," I continued. "Early heresies were settled by this very term 'Mother of God', since the church recognized and proclaimed that Jesus was fully God even in the womb."

"Mary is a nobody in the Bible," John continued.

"From *beginning to end,* Mary is inextricably linked in God's plan and the gospel," I said.

"She's got nothing to do with the gospel, except a little mention!"

"Says who, John, you? Scripture commences and concludes with Mary's role. Look at Genesis 3:15, which the early church called the *protoevangelion,* the first gospel."

In no time Fraser had flipped to it in his Bible and started reading it loudly for us: "I will put enmity between you and the woman, and between your offspring and her offspring; he shall bruise your head, and you shall bruise his heel."

"One verse," remarked John.

"John, this verse contains the hope of the ages. This prophecy relating to the defeat of the serpent (Satan) is found right at the start of Scripture, and announces the Messiah's victory over the devil through the 'crushing' of his head – the very seat of his pride. This is the first gospel, and it's inextricably linked with the 'woman', since it is her 'seed' or 'offspring' which crushes the enemy's head."

"Duh," said Fraser. "It's speaking about Eve."

"He's right," said John. "Where is Mary in this?"

"Mary is clearly foreshadowed in this."

"How's that?"

"Let me explain," I said, getting frustrated with their constant interruptions.

"Let him finish, then," said Rab.

"Eve is not called Eve ('life') until after this is announced – see Genesis 3:20 – since she would become the mother of every living person. But whose own son, 'offspring', was it that crushed the head of the serpent? Mary's son."

And so it continued. We fought our way from the "woman", "serpent", and "offspring" in Genesis 3 to the "woman", "serpent", and "offspring" in Revelation 12. I went on making a case from the Old Adam to the New Adam, and from the Old Eve to the New Eve, and pulled in others who were standing by, some of whom didn't agree with more basic doctrines, such as the divinity of Jesus.

Walking through the little huddle they had formed around me, I quoted Paul's commandment to Timothy concerning tradition: "O Timothy, guard the deposit entrusted to you. Avoid the irreverent babble and contradictions of what is falsely called 'knowledge', for by professing it some have swerved from the faith. Grace be with you" (1 Timothy 6:20–21).

Regrettably, I stopped trying to win by loving my brothers and began trying to win arguments with them; I became entrenched in my own views to the exclusion of all else. I settled for my own views and allowed a pride into my heart through which I became certain that "we" – the Roman Catholic Church – were the only Church to have the Holy Spirit. *We* were the only Church that were blessed by God; everything else was either a cult or a form of man-made gatherings. I still enjoyed going along to the different church meetings, but now I began to sit above them. I became extremely defensive.

Around this time a new minister took up the post as chaplain in HMP Glenochil. He was a passionate evangelical Baptist pastor, with a sharp mind and a passion for God and His word. His name was Graham Bell. Immediately, I clashed with him. I felt he did not represent the truth, and I had several heated discussions with him on Scripture, Catholicism, and other matters. I was convinced that these evangelicals were seriously mistaken, and that their *sola scriptura* was another way of saying what they wanted – while misusing the Bible to do so – and it made me harden my heart.

Then, while heading to a Prison Listener meeting, I arrived to see that Graham Bell was there representing the chaplaincy. There was only one seat left in the room and it was next to Graham. Reluctantly I sat next to him and, rather annoyed, I began to take my pen and paper out for the meeting. Suddenly, I sensed the familiar witness of the Holy Spirit, and I noticed that there was a power flowing out from Graham – the clean, familiar power of the Holy Ghost. I could feel the presence of God over him, and I was deeply affected by this. I wanted to question the Lord: "What, even them?" But the power and presence of God over the man made me repent of my arrogance and desire unity with my brothers again.

Although at the time of this meeting with Graham I was perplexed, and though I would have perhaps favoured staying within my own personal theological framework, I became so thankful to God for sending Graham to Glenochil, as he moved in the power of the Holy Ghost. Over time, he became my friend, brother, and mentor.

So it was that, through God's grace working in Graham, I became more interested in the Evangelical movement, especially the movements of the Holy Spirit within Evangelical history. I read about the revivals in Lewis and Wales, and how God swept mightily through communities, bringing them to true repentance and an awareness of Christ. I read writings and biographies concerning men of God from that tradition. I read about

Wesley and Whitefield, and about different individuals within the broad Evangelical movement, from Calvinists like Edwards and the great awakenings in the USA, to Wigglesworth and the birth of the Pentecostal movement. I marvelled at the mighty acts of God therein and rejoiced that God had not left me in my pride. It would have kept me within the narrow confines of my own views and robbed me of the glorious acts of the Holy Spirit who, like the wind, "blows where it wishes" (John 3:8).

Now two passions burned within me: evangelism and ecumenism – reaching those who are without Christ and without hope, and also seeking fellowship and reconciliation with my separated brothers in the body of Christ. Always, I took care to maintain my Catholic identity while pursuing fellowship in the Holy Spirit. I am not talking here about a false kind of ecumenism where truth is relative and everyone has their cake and eats it, which we see too often. It is apparent today among many Catholics that we have lost our sense of mission and urgency in sharing the gospel. Dialogue for dialogue's sake, flowing from a soteriological agnosticism (an uncertainty about those who are saved), has won the day. Whether in ecumenism or evangelism, the words of the apostle Paul should be seared onto the hearts of every baptized Catholic: "Woe to me if I do not preach the gospel!" (1 Corinthians 9:16). How can we but call men and women, here and now, to love and worship Jesus? He is the one who went to the agony of the cross for us – not just as a prophet, an enlightened one, but as the True God who alone can save. "There is salvation in no one else, for there is no other name under heaven given among men by which we must be saved" (Acts 4:12).

13

Life or Death

HMP Glenochil

I was beginning to feel intense sensations around my heart. I had no idea what was happening, but I could discern that these strange feelings were of a spiritual nature. In one moment I was in agony, then just when the pain became too much to bear, it burst into feelings of intense pleasure. An agony and ecstasy was playing out in my heart and I had no control over it. I was familiar with the feelings of peace and joy that the Holy Spirt sometimes refreshes us with, but here was something that was completely unexperienced. I sensed that God was going to show me something, yet when nothing came except the continual pains then pleasure, I was perplexed. What exactly was it?

I picked up the Bible and began flicking through its pages for some text to leap out at me for some reason or other. Yet there was nothing. The feelings increased, and

I had to sit down. I began to make involuntary groans, one minute from pain then the next from ecstasy. Then an intense burning began in my heart such as I have never experienced before. The sensation was neither pain nor pleasure, just an awareness of a spiritual fire in my heart.

"Oh God, what is it?" I prayed. "Oh, Lord."

I started saying my Rosary but found the intensity of the sensation overwhelming, and my vocal prayer turned into deep groans. In the distance I could hear the prison officers moving along the wing unlocking the cell doors for recreation. I worried that if these feelings didn't subside, people would see me and think I was completely crazy. As the screws came closer I jumped onto my bed and pretended to be asleep. They just opened the door, looked in, and walked on. The feelings waned a little and I felt confident enough to walk outside the door.

As soon as I walked out, the person in the cell next to me accidentally bumped into me. "Alright, Tony. Here's a paper," he said.

I took it, a little startled, and read. Suddenly I became aware of what God wanted me to see, and my heart sank. John MacDonagh, the person who had been responsible for setting up my friend Matt, had been shot dead in Glasgow in broad daylight. As I read the words of the newspaper describing the cold-blooded killing and how John had died begging for his life, my heart broke. I heard clearly the voice of God which has echoed through the ages, "I have set before you life and death, blessing and curse. Therefore choose..." (Deuteronomy 30:19). Perhaps the ecstasy that I experienced symbolises the sheer pleasure God has when we choose Christ, who is life and the way of blessing. The agony may also correspond to the anguish of God when his children choose death and remain in the curse.

Exactly one year after John MacDonagh had set Matt up, he had been killed. I trembled as I thought about the fate of the man. I knew from the verse God had spoken that He was showing me that John's fate would have been my fate, had I continued in the way I was going in the path of the curse. Through God's grace I had chosen a new way, the way of Christ, the way of blessing. I shuddered as I considered what might have happened had I stuck the screwdriver in John's neck, A year ago I had been on the brink of killing him when Matt's wounds made me consider Christ and stopped me in my tracks.

I went into my cell and wept. I began asking God to use me to bring souls back to Him. I wept bitterly for John and for all the other souls who do not know Jesus and are consequently heading for a lost eternity.

***

After five years in prison I could go for parole. It transpired that I had spent almost half my time in the chaos of stabbings, slashings, attacks on officers, smuggling, and all manner of disruption, not to mention fifteen months in solitary, as well as being reclassified an adult and booted out of the YOs. After I had committed my life to Christ, I did not even have a misconduct report (something which can be picked up for sleeping in in the morning). Instead, now I was a Prison Listener and a full-time participant of the education department, and I attended every church meeting. I had also gained some qualifications.

Some of the cons were keen to give me some advice as my parole date approached.

"Tony, don't go and tell them you've met Jesus and you're all better now," said Bill.

"Yeah. Loads of people have tried that and it doesn't work," added Paul.

"I am not going to tell them it was their 'cognitive skills' or their 'anger management'. Jesus has awakened in me the faith I had as child, and called me to walk in the newness of life He's given."

"Don't be daft!" said Paul. "This is your life, man!"

"Seriously," interrupted Bill, "Tell them in such a way as to make them think the system has broken you, changed you, you know, like you were a confused and disturbed individual, prone to feeling isolated and alienated by others, and your antisocial lifestyle and violence was a result of the rejection you felt after continually seeking acceptance yet never finding a place in society."

"No chance. "

"Tony, this is serious, man. Play your cards right and you could be out in a couple of months."

I was touched by their genuine concern but alarmed at the thought of not witnessing to Christ when it would matter most. How could I let the prison system claim it had rehabilitated me?

"Lads, I'll be telling the social workers doing my reports for the board that Jesus has given me a new heart."

"You're mental" said Paul.

"Good luck with that!" added Bill.

They stared at me in disbelief, as if I was from another planet.

"Thanks for the advice, lads, but even if it means getting more jail time, I'll be telling them that it was Jesus who changed me."

I returned to my cell, and I smiled as I realized I

was *sitting* in the cell. Actually sitting. For years of my sentence I could not sit. I had had no peace; I would pace back and forth, back and forth, tormented and haunted by a life of heinous acts. Now it was so nice to have peace. The truth was that my prison was no prison now I had Christ in my life. I had His peace, and the freedom of the children of God – a far greater freedom than many experience outside of prison. I looked back at the carnage and violence of those early years, the continual psychological, as well as physical, fights. Now the anxiety and stress were all gone. I could not say anything other than that Christ had freed me.

I asked the chaplain, "Graham, will you pray with me?"

"What's up?"

"My parole!"

"Sure," he said. "How are you feeling about it?"

"Kinda just wanna witness, but I'd love to get out there and start serving God."

"Anthony, He is able."

We prayed and committed it to God.

***

The day came for the social worker to begin doing my reports, but she wanted to meet with me and take preliminary notes. She was a short, young woman in her late twenties, with a short haircut and a stern face. She sat down and immediately began asking questions without looking at me, as she raked in her handbag for a pen.

"So what are you in for again?" she asked, looking for her file.

"Attempted murder," I replied.

"Can you tell me about that?"

"Yes, but... but do you not have the details in your report?"

"I want you to tell me about it."

"I'd rather not."

"Why are you being uncooperative?"

"I'm not... it's... well... I've not thought about it in so long."

"Was it easy for you to forget?"

"That's not what I mean."

"Ah here it is. Samurai swords, I see." She was determined to go over every detail of that night.

My heart sank. How was it I had done such a thing? My thoughts flew apart and I wanted to leave the small room as she read everything out loud.

"Look, I am not that person any more."

"Your prison records are interesting, too. I see you have even added to your criminal record while in prison."

"Yes but that was before I changed. That's who I used to be. I... I... I'm now a Christian, and I'm different," I managed to stutter.

"Righhht," she said, with a prolonged, cynical tone.

The rest of the meeting was a blur as I tried to answer as best as I could and force the terrible memories away from me.

***

"How did it go?" asked Graham as I returned to my cell.

"It was awful. I couldn't explain anything. Anyway I don't deserve my parole; I'm an animal," I said, holding back tears of remorse. *How could I have done such things?*

"Deserve…" he repeated thoughtfully. "You're right, you don't deserve your parole. If it comes down to what we deserve, none of us would be here."

"Eh?"

"Anthony, God has given us grace. Do you even know what grace is?"

"Divine assistance to humanity," I said, quoting Augustine in a dry, speculative manner.

"Yes," he said rather exhaustedly, "but it's also God's undeserved favour. It's not earned. In God's eyes, 'None is righteous, no, not one', [Romans 3:10], 'for all have sinned and fall short of the glory of God' [Romans 3:23]. *All* means *all:* everyone, without exception, falls beneath the standard God requires, whether it be the sweet old lady who has committed no crime during her life, or the guy on death row. All are in need of the grace of God. For although a person may not have committed a 'great crime,' undoubtedly they will have sinned in word, deed, or thought, and 'the wages of sin is death' [Romans 6:23]. That means eternal separation from God. This is why God sent His Son into the world, to take upon Himself the sin of the world. Through faith in Him, we receive the grace of justification – of being declared right with God – and sanctification – of being made holy."

Graham was always quick to remind me, in such simple and beautiful ways, that the great hope we have is all undeserved. After a time of prayer, he left, and I began to ask God with all my heart to release me from prison. I asked Him to overrule from heaven all human judgment relating to my release. I was desperate to get out and share the gospel with others.

The day arrived for the final assessment that would sum up everything and determine whether or not I was "safe" to go back into society. Providentially, the cynical social worker was off sick and a Christian social worker was sent to do the final report that would go to the parole board. This lady, after hearing me say, "Jesus has changed me", asked to hear my full testimony. Shortly after this, I was released from prison. God's grace and mercy had triumphed over judgment.

I went forth to greet both triumph and disaster, great mistakes and great miracles, called, as it were, to walk upon the water, knowing that whenever the wind and the waves of sin caused me to sink, the sacrament of confession would help me to take His hand. Then Jesus would be swift to lift me back up and, with His own body and blood, strengthen me for the journey ahead…

14

Liberation

"Anthony, are you a chav?" asked one brother from the order, who saw no problem with his manner of inquiry. I could see it was a novel experience for them to have a member of the community wearing a tracksuit and trainers. My accent and manner of speaking set me apart even more, and I struggled to fit in. But I honestly didn't know any better. No matter how kind and patient I tried to be, still the hurts kept coming, and the constant drip of discouragement wore me down. I asked myself constantly, how did I end up here?

***

After being released from jail, I summoned my will and fixed it on serving God. I would allow nothing to get in the way or distract me. Nothing. Yet this was easier said than done. My old friends were showing up in the middle of the night to offer me £20,000 "just to see you on your feet". At the same time, my family, who had fallen on brutal times, were buying yellow label food items from Asda and filling the freezer with them to prevent them from rotting. But I would not let these things hinder me. Through God's grace I perceived all these traps and avoided them... for now, anyway.

I was "home", yet I could not have felt any more like an alien. Well-meaning friends and family members had waited five years for Tony to return, but Anthony had arrived instead. I had insisted on being called Anthony right after my experience with the Holy Spirit. Back in that solitary cell, obeying an inner impulse, I wrote on a piece of paper "Anthony", and also "Thank Ian Frazor." Years later it transpired that an old family friend called Ian Frazor had prayed unceasingly for me. God had also given me what I so longed for in the name "Anthony", since it represented a new nature and was the name given in Holy Baptism. Interestingly, it was only other Christians who would call me Anthony. Anyway, I strove with all my heart to live out this new nature and put Tony more and more to death.

I could see no better way of doing this than by joining a strict Catholic order, and there was one I so wanted to join. And so, after only a couple of months out of prison, I travelled to England to join a community and consider perpetual vows of poverty, chastity, and obedience. Filled with the thoughts of St Francis, St Dominic and St Louis de Montfort, I was overjoyed that I had been permitted to join the community for a postulancy (candidacy) period. I longed for nothing more than to renounce earthly possessions, devote myself to Christ in chastity, and obey His representatives as if they were Christ Himself.

On my arrival, I was stunned. I expected to see a community united around the rule of their founder, obeying orders with military precision, practising poverty with their renunciation of wealth and status, and striving to put purity into action. How my soaring ideals were about to be shattered! I was shocked to see that the order now lived in a mansion – far, it seemed to me, from the poor with whom they were supposed to be "totally identified", according to their founder's strict instructions. Sadly, there was also no obedience. As far as I could tell, there were sharp divisions and strong individuality, and some priests even insisted on having their own properties nearby, producing an environment akin to hotel living. All of the above were clear breaches of the rules by which the order had been established.

I was immediately placed with the other young men. They were so different from me. They were very refined and some were already well on their way to becoming priests. The first thing I noticed was how well educated they were. At mealtimes I struggled to make conversation. Though I had memorized Scripture and committed the stories of the saints to heart, this was considered childish in comparison to modern theologians and existential philosophies, and so I often sat silently in ignorance. However, still fresh from the fire of conversion, during our free time I was desperate to speak with people about God. I tried to talk about Jesus, Scripture, saints, just anything to do with God. Unwittingly, I wearied the others so much that a complaint was made to the Superior about me, with one brother stating bluntly, "I need a break from him, I don't want to talk about Jesus all the ***** time."

I became more and more isolated and would spend all my free time in the chapel, but this irritated the others even more. I was called in by the Superior and warned about "acting better than others". But I had no friends and did not fit in, and rather than feel inadequate all the time, I found relief in Jesus' company.

Even when we were invited to the houses of the parishioners, I found it brutal. (The parish was situated in one of the richest areas in England). It's sad that the way a person holds their knife and picks their food up with a fork can leave them socially labelled, and sadder still when this happens among a community brought together under the cross of Christ. So it was that my table manners gave me away. By now I was starting to become ashamed of my manner of speaking and would try to be as quiet as possible. Then the table would have conversations about me, as if I was not there. There would be comments, such as, "I bet he is a deep thinker really." They made jokes about me in my presence. When we met for community prayer I couldn't read music or even simple psalm tones for the chant, which really annoyed the blossoming musicians.

When Christmas 2008 came, the postulants were permitted to go home, but I had no money and I would not ask my family for any, so I remained alone as the others within the community went off. Nobody else remained, and so I took myself back to the chapel. That Christmas passed slowly.

Gradually, I suspected the community were becoming ashamed of me, and I began to believe that my acceptance into the order had only been a result of the pressure of finding priests. These suspicions were compounded after a "vocations day", a time for people who are considering a religious vocation (such as priests, monks, and nuns) to come and hear the stories of those who have already taken the first step. Thus we, as postulants preparing for the priesthood, were asked to share our stories. I so looked forward to this occasion as the vocations day was to be held in Paisley, Scotland, where I would not have to worry too much about my accent and manner of speaking. But on the morning of the day I was taken aside and asked not to share. This devastated me. The really hurtful thing was that I had planned to speak more about our founder's example and not my background. I had the sense to see that my past was now a scandal.

After eight months I was one of only a few postulants left. The others, unsatisfied with this and that, had found that their constant criticisms of the programme, the priests, and the lack of pay had paved for them a path home. Now I was suddenly being treated courteously and respectfully. I found it strange, but clearly the community were keen to hang on to what was left, even if it was the thickly accented, ex-con chav from Scotland.

Now all of this would have been gladly endured had the gospel not been so disdainfully cast aside. My love of this order, no matter how deep, would not supplant my love of the gospel. It became unbearable to me when I considered that the very purpose of our vows was to make us obedient to the call of Christ and His commission to bring all into His saving work. Time after time, when I suggested outreach, I was dismissed.

My phone calls home simultaneously broke my heart and burdened me even more for mission, since my family would update me on which of my friends back home were now dead from overdoses, suicides, and shootings, all while I sat within the safe, comfortable walls of the order. Then one day I heard our director boasting of how he had refused to let one of the refugees they were looking after hear the story of another refugee who had found Christ. In fact, out of "respect" for the other Muslim refugees, this person who had turned to Christ had been expelled.

At this I left so quickly that I abandoned my most treasured possessions – my books! All the books my family had scrimped to buy me were left there. Along with my Bible, I carried away just two books with me, seemingly contradictory in nature on account of their different theological outlooks. However, they serve as a good indication of the theological currents that continued to shape me. One book was a little biography of the Pentecostal revivalist Smith Wigglesworth, and the other was *The Secret of the Rosary* by Louis de Montfort. I remained a strange mix of conservative and charismatic Catholicism.

It would be unfair to say that everything was bad in the order. There were two very beautiful people that I had come to know. One was Fr Dermott and another was Fr David. Fr Dermott always demonstrated such a love of the poor that he inspired and edified all who came into contact with him. At times I also heard him defending me when others were complaining or mocking my dress sense. Fr David was another good man who, on noticing my lack of confidence around others, would take me down to the chapel late at night, away from the others, and teach me to overcome my fears. He also taught me how to ensure the congregation got the most out of the readings through good, intentional delivery. There was so much I was able to learn from these men, and I am extremely grateful for the experience. They were a constant consolation and remain in my memory as a treasure.

When I returned to Edinburgh, I was both relieved and discouraged; filled with hope yet extremely weary.

How I still longed to reach my friends and family with the gospel. However, discipleship would now have to be continued in the context of "the world", and however difficult I had found things within the safety of the cloister, it had still served as a mighty breaker from the waves of the world. It was a torment to live in Edinburgh. It seemed that every day I was trying to avoid old friends and situations – and many times, to my horror, I failed.

Having been a plumber prior to going to prison, I began a small company called AJG Plumbing Services. I remember clearing a lot of money after receiving and completing the contract for two new builds in Edinburgh. Yet money did not motivate me at all. All I wanted to do, longed to do, was to serve God and my neighbour to the fullest. While plumbing and Christian service are not mutually exclusive, I sensed deeply the need to study in order to be the best I could be for the gospel.

While praying about my "vocation", and burdened deeply about my sins and sense of failure in light of all God had done for me, I walked out to the fields. After I had been praying for some time, I suddenly heard a bird singing. There was something about its piercing melody that made me cease my confused complaints to God and, laughing loudly, I praised Him for such beauty.

Later that day, while my friend Graham was praying for me, he suddenly turned and said, "God wants you to simply to listen to the birds singing and trust Him." Now no one had known about my experience earlier in the morning; I had not discussed it with anyone.

Further to my discussions with Graham and my friends in Stirling, it was suggested that I consider attending a theological college in Glasgow (International Christian College). After looking at what it offered I was desperate to attend, if only to study God's word at a deeper level and be enabled to make the connections, as the college proclaimed, "between God's word and God's world".

Arrangements were made for me to move to Stirling. I was so desperate to leave Edinburgh, knowing how weak I really was and acknowledging that the place was another Egypt, pulling my soul back into slavery, that I dropped my nets (van and tools) and fled. My friend Scott gladly took them up, free of charge, for his own construction business.

Arrangements were made for me to live with a Dr Stuart Reid. I worried about this and really wondered if St Ninians Community in Stirling had lost their mind, placing an ex-prisoner with an astrophysicist. How wrong I was. Dr Stuart Reid was a really passionate evangelical who took me in, refusing rent and welcoming me as I was. Unlike my experience with the community in England, Stuart could not have been any kinder. He demonstrated such patience and kindness that I found myself continually blessing God for the help and discipleship I received at his hands. Although extremely intelligent, he never belittled or looked down on me, and never was I made to feel ashamed of the way I spoke or dressed. Rather, Stuart was a continual reminder of the kindness of God demonstrated through His committed people. I lived there for almost three years before moving to Glasgow. Never have I seen kindness like Dr Reid's.

After completing an application for ICC and attending an interview, I was enrolled in August 2009 only a few months after returning from England. I had gone from a Catholic order to an Evangelical institution – two contrasting settings. However, ICC was really like coming home. I seemed to be surrounded by people who were passionate about the gospel and reaching others with the message of salvation. Every class seemed to blend academic excellence with practical application. Almost all of the students and lecturers were committed Christian men and women intent on spreading the kingdom of God. I seemed to have found the heartbeat of Jesus within the college's walls, and with every beat I heard "evangelism". During the classes, our lecturers encouraged us to think for ourselves, refusing to let denominationalism get in the way of what God was asking of *His* students. Rather than being told *what* to think, we were taught *how* to think. We were presented with almost every theological perspective and asked to think for ourselves as they trained us to rightly handle God's word.

I rejoiced to find so many Catholic authors on our reading lists. Furthermore, while I was the only Catholic in the college, lecturers made use of the writings of St John of the Cross, St Ignatius of Loyola, and St John Paul II, and encouraged us to review the documents of the Second Vatican Council. So it was that within this Evangelical setting, my Catholic faith was being nourished and encouraged in way that totally outdid the order I had considered joining. Interestingly, I found that the deeper the theological issues, the more other Christian scholarship not only consulted but also depended on Catholic thought to navigate between culture and Christ. From hermeneutics to bioethics, as well as missions and marriage, I found great assurance and repose in the *regula fidei.*

There were, of course, significant disagreements between myself and other students, but this was not confined to the Catholic/Evangelical debates. In ICC there were Charismatics and Conservatives, Calvinists and Arminians, but there was often such a bond of love transcending these disputes that even heated debates served only to sharpen, awaken, and dispel ignorance on both sides. Debates often continued between students for days, and would end with a prayer meeting and a lunch. I felt genuinely caught up in a work of the Spirit that was bringing Christians into an experience of deep unity. This was only reinforced when I considered the college in the context of Glasgow and the bitter sectarianism that has dogged the city.

At ICC I formed friendships that I am so thankful to God for, particularly my friends David and John, with whom I met regularly to read Scripture and pray, as well as keep each other accountable as we pursued Christ with all our hearts. I look back on my friendship with these men and remember an intellectual experience that was as refreshing as pure mountain air. We would challenge one another to an ever deeper discipleship through rigorous Scripture study. There were many nights when we stayed up, sitting side by side, translating the New Testament from the original Greek, clause after clause, line after line, poring over original texts, parsing with passion and translating for treasures.

***

It happened as I slipped into class late. Taking a seat at the back of the lecture hall close to a wall, so as to see and not be seen, I noticed a girl with red hair. I quickly dismissed the notions arising within me as foolish. Yet providence would weave a pattern that brought us closer, and through group discussions on evangelism and mission, this girl became even more attractive.

One day I was invited to share my testimony by some friends of mine who had turned a broken-down bar in one of the most notorious areas of Glasgow into a place for the broken. I had come to know the place after I had helped to refit the plumbing when it had been broken into and the copper pipes stolen. I invited some of my friends from ICC along, knowing many of them would be blessed to see what God was now doing in a bar that had formerly witnessed murders.

Halfway through my testimony, one of the gangs from the area broke through a newly patched outer wall and hurled a brick at me. As I stopped, I asked the assembly to pray for them. As we prayed, we were immersed in the presence of God, and later I was able to witness to these lads.

After I spoke, I noticed that the girl with the red hair had come along. We started chatting that evening and got to know each other a little better. Her name was Anna and, finding she had a passion for the lost and a powerful testimony of God's goodness, I fell head over heels in love with her. Anna and I formed a friendship and began to spend more and more time together.

Looking back, this was also a very challenging time for me, as I found Anna's organized personality and realism difficult. My lofty, unrealistic ideals were often brought crashing to the ground by Anna's practical and realistic observations. She also challenged my disorganization and lack of punctuality – to no avail – thus there were challenges felt on both sides! Nevertheless, it was good that this starry-eyed idealist met with a determined pragmatist.

As I finished my third year at ICC, I was invited to a meeting with the academic registrar and the vice-principal. I was delighted when they told me that my grades meant I could continue on to a fourth year as an honours student. I felt I had neglected my studies at times in favour of outreach on the streets: every weekend Anna and I would take soup around the streets for the homeless, as well as clothing and information on where they could find help. Both Anna and I had received the college's award for excellence in practical theology two years in a row. However, my studies had suffered as a result.

The vice-principal Dr Miller said, "Anthony, the poor you will always have with you. It's time to not let your studies suffer any more." I should have taken better heed. I had great respect for Dr Miller. Throughout my time at ICC, no matter how busy he was, he always took the time to offer support and, whether academic or pastoral, he was a great encouragement. Looking back, I don't think I could have finished my training without his guidance.

15

Follow Me

"Stop taking Jesus to the market place. FOLLOW HIM!" shouted the preacher, staring straight at me. He then went on emphasize Jesus' invitation: "Follow me." These words shook me to the core.

The next day, Anna and I took a walk over to Glasgow's necropolis, as was our custom at study breaks or lunch, when suddenly, some way up the street, I noticed a man bowed low, sitting hunched on a fence. He looked so burdened. Rather than just go over to speak with him, as would be my usual approach, I determined to follow Jesus and so I stopped and prayed: "God, if you would like me to talk to him, make him look up at me." He was a good way up the road with his head twisted in the other direction. As soon as I opened my eyes, he turned right around and started to stare at me. Anna had been praying the very same thing. So we set off in his direction to see if we could help in any way.

Suddenly, I heard the screech of brakes and car horns amid shouts and swearing. A scary-looking man, covered in tattoos, with the sides of his head shaved and huge, spiky punk tufts running along the middle of his skull, had run through the traffic. He grabbed me forcefully, saying two words: "Follow me."

He was very intimidating and, had it not been for the preacher's message the previous day which still burned within me, I would have shrugged his arm off. Yet I was compelled by the words "Follow me", and so I did. Anna went off to see the other man while I went with this strange individual. A few moments later he had taken me to his lair where he lived, under Glasgow's Royal Hospital.

The epitome of the anarchist, his arms were covered in tattoos and bangles made from snapped Mercedes badges. In his denims, boots, and ripped T-shirt he still held me by the arm, pulling me along behind him. "Come on, this is where I live."

We travelled down a dark, old, Victorian stairwell. "Watch out for that!" he said, pointing to a piece of polystyrene lying on the ground at the foot of the stairs. "It's a trap." This man had strategically placed it over a manhole at the entry point to his prime pitch where it menacingly awaited any unwanted intruders. Below the polystyrene there was a four-foot drop, at the bottom of which were broken bottles and glass.

He welcomed me into his "palace", where he had cleverly used the backdraught from two huge boilers to blow hot air continuously through his sleeping quarters. I could see that this was one of Glasgow's write-offs – a hopeless alcoholic by the look of all the empty bottles outside his pitch, and probably a violent drunk, by the look of his broken and scraped knuckles. He was a determined scavenger, forcefully taking the crumbs from others' tables. Yet despite having noticed this, I had a heartfelt connection to him and, through gentleness, his fiercely proud exterior was overcome. I saw a man before me who had received from society both rejection and charity, yet he was clearly craving justice.

"My name is John, and I wasn't always like this," he said, looking down, embarrassed.

John allowed me to take him food and clothing when I could. Then, after arranging to see him one day, I found I was unable to go, owing to a fast-approaching essay deadline I had overlooked. I asked some other Christian students from ICC to see John and take some food to him. "But most of all pray for him," I asked.

Later in the evening they returned, telling me eagerly, "After we prayed for him, John decided that he would not take another drink."

I thanked them for all their kindness and quickly excused myself before rushing to the graveyard where John spent his time, greatly concerned about the effects of a sudden withdrawal from alcohol. When I arrived, John excitedly told me how he had poured away the last of his alcohol. He wouldn't listen to any of my warnings about the dangers of abruptly giving it up. So I felt compelled to take him home with me, sneaking him into the student halls of Bible College and right into my room. I had to keep watch over him through what I feared could be a deadly night.

What followed were days of horrendous alcohol withdrawals. The smell emanating from my room became so bad that I had to ask Anna to go up and down the corridor outside spraying air freshener in order to hide our unofficial guest. I lived in a single room and had snuck a mattress in for John to sleep on my floor. It was crazy, and I could have been kicked out of the Bible College because of it.

Gradually, it became more and more difficult to hide the situation, and eventually I was found out by the two wardens responsible for the student halls. However, rather than giving me the anticipated rebuke, with the usual talking to about "being sensible" and keeping others and their belongings safe, the two wardens, both of whom had been through the Christian Teen Challenge rehabilitation programme for addictions, graciously offered their support in finding alternative accommodation for John. Not only did they offer their support, but they also helped to organize a whip-round among the other students, who by now had become aware of the situation. Between all of us, we got together enough money for a month's deposit and rent.

Amid lectures and deadlines, not to mention the fact that Anna and I had decided to get married but had no house to move into after marriage, no jobs, and a wedding to plan, we set about letting tomorrow worry about itself and getting on with the day's problems – finding John accommodation and stability.

After visiting several properties in Glasgow – all of which proved difficult, as some letting agents turned their noses up at this potential tenant while others greedily tried to extort more money for damp, mouldy, dilapidated flats – I'd had enough. I was rushing to get back for a lecture and there were essays due left, right, and centre. I became so frustrated at the way the housing system could treat people. As I was pulling up to a red light, I remember banging my fists on the steering wheel and asking God, "Who is there in your church that could help? There must be someone."

There just had to be somebody. The situation had become untenable and I could no longer keep sneaking

John back to the halls. Yet I could not abandon him now that he had committed himself to Christ. At that moment a name flew through my mind: Roy Lees. I remembered Roy as a man who had a heart for addicts. Even if he couldn't help, I knew he would give me the best advice. Then and there, I pulled the car over to the side of the road and called Roy.

"Roy, how are you? It's Anthony here."

"Hey Anthony, what's up?"

"I've got an alcoholic who has secretly detoxed in my bedroom in Bible College. I have nowhere to place him and time is running out. He has nowhere else to go and has committed his life to Christ."

Roy laughed hysterically and told me he'd call me right back. Minutes later the phone rang and Roy gave me the name and number of a man called David Black, a Christian landlord on the west of Scotland. I thanked Roy for his help and phoned the number he had given me.

David Black was a man I had previously come to know through Christian circles. He was a man with a big heart who believed in a big God. After my discussion with David on the phone, a meeting was arranged between us and, after a few more days of plate-spinning, the day of the meeting came and I prepared to find out whether a home could be found for our friend.

At the meeting, David explained that he was the chairman of an organization that offered help and support to those recovering from addiction. He talked about the necessity of a programme for those who are in recovery and that, while John had a lot to learn, he also had a lot to unlearn, and programmes such as the one David was involved in could really help. However, like a father that grants a son's request, yielding to his love more than the wisdom of his experience, he offered us a home for John.

Later, as he showed us round the lovely flat he had for John, he just "happened" to mention a flat he had down the road and asked if we would like to see it. Straight away I could see what was happening. David was playing it smart as he took us to the other flat. He was looking for a "married couple" to move in to it, and before I could say anything, Anna was on her way down the street.

As we entered the house, David moved over to the French windows of the small living room and, pulling the curtains apart, he revealed the most stunning view I have ever seen. Both Anna and I gasped as the dramatic Clyde estuary met the rugged majesty of Scotland's west coast mountains.

Anna stated, "This would be a lovely first home."

I quickly replied, "We'll have to pray about it."

David laughed, knowing that his work was done. We now had a home to go to after our marriage.

***

Three weeks prior to our wedding day, I had been visiting our new home-to-be in Port Glasgow, doing little touch-ups, paintwork, and odds and ends around the house, and popping by to visit John whose new home was just a few doors away. He seemed to be settling in happily, and we had helped him to make connections with local Christians who were treating him well. However, John was still quite isolated, and I worried about idleness leading to relapse.

Around this time I was invited to the Isle of Jura with some of Anna's family to attend a wedding. John asked if he could be of any help in getting the flat ready while I was away, as he had seen how hard I had been working to make sure everything was right for Anna to move in after our marriage. I thanked John and left some instructions before setting off to Jura.

While I was heading to Jura, I received a job offer from David Black, and I marvelled at God's kindness, and the authority of Christ's words, "But seek first the kingdom of God and his righteousness, and all these things will be added to you" (Matthew 6:33). Through trying to help another man, which had only been obedience to the words "Follow me", I had gone from having no house and no job right into a job teaching the Bible to addicts, as well as having a home that was geographically positioned at the opposite end of the country from Edinburgh – my personal Egypt.

Anna and I, along with her brother, returned after a wonderful time in Jura, to pay a flying visit to our flat and check on progress. The house that had been well on its way to becoming our first happy home, a place where we could move in together after our marriage, had been destroyed. While we were away, an ex-girlfriend of John's had reappeared, and with her came the chains of addiction. Now our new home, and even our new neighbourhood, had been thrown into chaos. The freshly painted walls of our flat were spattered with all manner of stains, from teabags stuck to the walls to blood stains from an obvious drunken fight. Our floors and beds had been used as ashtrays. Furthermore, John was so drunk and out of his mind that when I walked in he eagerly showed me how he had made a pea-shooter out of our curtain rail! We could see the evidence of this innovative implement all over the place. Our beautiful home now looked like a crack den.

Our neighbours reported that while we had been away the two of them had gone on a bender, fighting constantly, and at one point even threatening each other with blades. One of the Christian friends we had connected them to, a lovely gentle man called Donald, also reported walking into John's flat to find him slicing a tattooed name off his body!

Now the entire street was in an uproar about this pair and the "people" who had brought them there. Neighbourhood relations only plummeted further after John started a bonfire in the street using wood he had sourced from both his and other neighbours' fences.

At 7.30 a.m. the next day I found myself walking up a road not far from the ruined flat I'd been trying to clean and prepare for my future wife. Stress enveloped me as I contemplated my final Hebrew exams over the next few days, as well as how to prevent the neighbours from forming a lynch mob. All of this was on top of fathoming how to even begin getting the flat back into a habitable state before Anna and I would move in. I was at breaking point.

I returned home, and by the time I had finished my Rosary, light and clarity had entered; darkness and confusion had left. I realized that despite the change I had seen in John, he was still in great need of discipleship. What was I thinking, taking a homeless man who had spent most of his life on the street and simply dropping him into a flat and expecting him to get on with it? Somewhere I had read that "when a weak soul is converted, like a plant, it needs to be transplanted into fresh soil and given light and water along with time and a chance of true growth" (Padré Pio).

After much discussion, prayer, and persuasion, I made arrangements for John and Elenor, his girlfriend, to go into respective rehabs. John was so sad that he would not be able to attend my wedding that he took off his most prized possession, a battered and scraped silver ring, and gave it to me. In return I took off my own ring, which a friend had given me, and we swapped. John's ring would become my wedding ring, and I still wear it to this day.

And so the words "follow me" had taken me on a process of learning the great need for discipleship and ongoing conversion after any decision for Christ is made. I know this also from deep personal pain and bitter experience. But an awareness of my own sin and failures as a Christian only adds to a compassion for souls like John and Elenor. After all, how many times had I stained and ruined God's dwelling, the temple of His Spirit, through my own falls?

***

Since my conversion, my hands have never been raised against another person. God alone accomplished this, breaking the chains of hatred that held me. But what about the violence of my other sins, which flowed from disordered passions, chaotic emotions, a weakened will, and a darkened intellect?

Pope Benedict's words to us in Bellahouston Park in Glasgow on 16 September 2010 were sobering: "There are many temptations placed before you every day – drugs, money, sex, pornography, alcohol – which the world tells you will bring you happiness, yet these things are destructive and divisive."

Bitterly I have battled these temptations and many others, and I continue to battle them, but they keep turning up, fresh expressions of sin to avoid. But what about when failure finds me? What about when I have trashed my witness, wrecked my resolutions, wounded my neighbour through bad example, and placed stumbling blocks in front the weak? It is here that this testimony hinges. When overcome by my destructive inclinations I can testify to the reception of grace that conquers through genuine confession.

The soul resembles a pool that quickly becomes muddied and murky in its sins, whether in rebellion or weaknesses. If cleansing grace is not received, then the pool becomes darker, blocking the Son and destroying the life within it. Eventually the water turns foul and stagnant. Confession therefore can be compared to a God-given inlet of grace and outlet for darkness within the soul. True confession always obtains the grace of God, and this grace is poured forth so abundantly, and it is in this respect that the Sacrament of Reconciliation is a conduit of grace and an outlet for darkness. Shame, guilt, and all manner of crippling spiritual agonies are pushed out under the pressure of God's love, while grace powerfully pours into the soul. Then, like a pool flooded with fresh water, the soul starts to become cleaner and purer. All that is contained within begins to be seen clearly as darkness is pushed out. The smallest fault is magnified by the water's purity, which sharpens the sinner's focus as genuine sanctification is pursued.

While studying at ICC I rejoiced to find that among evangelicals there has dawned an awareness of the biblical position on confession (James 5:16; 1 John 1:9). For instance, Dietrich Bonhoeffer, one of the twentieth century's greatest evangelical theologians and himself a pastor, states:

In confession the break-through to community

takes place. Sin demands to have a man by himself. It withdraws him from the community. The more isolated a person is, the more destructive will be the power of sin over him, and the more deeply he becomes involved in it, the more disastrous is his isolation... In confession the light of the Gospel breaks into the darkness and seclusion of the heart.

In confession the break-through to new life occurs. Where sin is hated, admitted, and forgiven, there the break with the past is made.[3]

It is exactly this reconciliation to the community (the church) that has helped me, time after time, fall after fall, to pick myself up and carry on, knowing and claiming the assurance given to the apostles and their successors: "If you forgive the sins of any, they are forgiven them" (John 20:23). It is this sacrament that remains the gateway to the "source and summit"[4] of my faith, Jesus' real presence. It is the Sacrament of Confession that has made this testimony possible.

16

Nothing is Impossible

The best day of my life came on 1 July 2012 when I was united in the Sacrament of Marriage to the love of my life, Anna. I remember standing at the front of the church, palms sweaty, smiling through the nerves as I waited in the packed little church. Then she appeared, like grace personified. How I had longed for this day. Slowly she made her way down the aisle and we took our vows before God. I was now united to my best friend and fearless companion in the gospel. There are no words to describe the joy of that day.

The following year, on 15 June, I graduated from ICC with a theology degree from Aberdeen University. I chose not to do my honours year and resolved to work full-time with those in addiction at the Haven, Kilmacolm. At the Haven, I took up the post of overseeing the teaching and pastoral programme, and the real highlight was witnessing Christ work among the students. Throughout this time, I often felt the atmosphere was charged with the presence of God. I witnessed outpourings of the Spirit, healings, and deliverances from demons.

***

In the spring of 2014 Anna and I departed from a sad appointment with a doctor who had just informed us that it was "impossible" for us to have children. The reason for this lay in the difficulty Anna had endured years earlier – before I knew her – when she had been informed, just prior to her nineteenth birthday, that she had a brain tumour as well as two other tumours – one at the top of her spine and another at the base of her spine. The cancer was only discovered after several years of excruciating back pain. Not only did the cancer rob her of her childhood dream of becoming a doctor, as the treatment had made it too difficult for her to return to study medicine; now, from what this specialist said, her dream of motherhood was also shattered.

As we prepared to return to work at the Haven, having just nipped out for an afternoon appointment, we prayed and wiped the tears from our eyes. Then, after inwardly recalling all that the doctor had said, I suddenly heard clearly in my spirit a Scripture, followed by a reference. It was strange since not only did I hear the words, "Thus saith the Lord, I will yet for this be inquired of", but it was followed by a specific reference, chapter and verse, as I also heard, "Ezekiel 36:37." Startled, I suggested to Anna that we stop for a coffee and a little time to compose ourselves before returning to work. At times, hope comes hard, and makes one wary of sharing too soon with another whose heart has just been the anvil for the hammer. Anna's grief in that moment was far greater than mine.

She sat sadly with her cup as I shared that I believed God wanted us to "inquire of him" concerning this news.

Anna encouraged me to look up the verse and, because the verse came in archaic English, I flipped to the King James Version option in my phone's Bible app. We both smiled as we read the reference in full: "Thus saith the Lord God; I will yet for this be inquired of by the house of Israel, to do it for them; I will increase them with men like a flock." Encouraged, we returned to the Haven with not a little hope kindled.

Not long after this Anna fell pregnant. Then in the twenty-fourth week of pregnancy, having casually gone along to the hospital expecting a simple solution to some of the slight pains she was feeling, we were informed that the baby was on his way. We already knew he was a boy, and we had named him Louis. "He's too little," Anna said, blinking through her tears. And so, with one hand holding hers tightly, my other was already searching for statistics on my phone. I trembled as I stared into this chalice. Barely a month earlier, my twin brother Michael had drunk to its bitter dregs, having laid to rest his beautiful baby boy Tighearnan, who had just suffered a cot death at ten months old.

Then after texting and calling in as much prayer as possible, a friend in Germany got in touch. Unbeknown to him, he was speaking to me from the very Scripture that I used so often to encourage the Haven students. It was from the valley of dry bones (Ezekiel 37), where God speaks to His helpless and hopeless people concerning His might and ability to deliver despite all odds and obstacles. Moreover, the verse came with great power and urgency along with much attention to detail that directly spoke into Louis' situation: the medics maintained great concern regarding Louis' lungs, skin, and body weight. Yet, "breath", "skin", and "tissue" were all wrapped up in a verse from the same prophet God had used to give us hope in the first place.

I would love to say, as Anna can, that I knew that familiar, unshakable peace that Christ often imparts to us in the midst of life's crosses. But despite the verses and the memories of God moving powerfully in my life, and having seen Him move so powerfully at the Haven, I experienced only stress and anxiety, which forced me to cling to the rock of Christ rather than rest on it.

Our baby boy Louis, named after St Louis de Montfort, was born on 7 October 2014 – the feast of the Holy Rosary! He was so tiny, a mere 1lb 10oz, all black and blue from the battering of labour at his tiny gestation. The nurse quickly picked him up and placed him in a little plastic bag in order to maintain heat and protect his frail skin. I could see his little mouth opening and closing, producing the faintest of little whimpers. He was quickly taken away by the medics, and though we had received such encouragement and signs of God's favour, still panic pounded my heart.

A few hours later, the door of the room we were in flew open and our tiny baby was wheeled through, now more a pinkish colour and attached to a ventilator, with the doctor laughing and saying, "Someone needs to tell this baby he is only twenty-four weeks. What a fight I had with him…"

Louis had been wriggling and kicking so much, he had to be held down in order for breathing support to be offered. It was a good start to a long journey, and four months later our little boy was home and doing well.

Then, barely a year later, in September 2015, Anna was again admitted to the labour suite at Glasgow's Southern General, as our second baby, Peter, was on his way. This time he was coming at twenty-three weeks. The stats were even worse in Peter's case: only three out of ten babies make it at twenty-three weeks, but through God's mercy, Anna was enabled to hold on for ten days, taking Peter into what we believed was his twenty-fourth week. Although only an additional week, the statistics improved to a 50 per cent survival rate. Peter was born on 16 September 2015, and the doctor overseeing his delivery insisted she believed he was gestationally younger: "Definitely within the twenty-three-week period!"

Peter's journey was as miraculous as Louis', and we believe his safe return home was only a result of prayer. At one crisis point, our Bishop called to inform us that five hundred children had just prayed for Peter at a school assembly. Many other faithful friends and church communities stormed heaven on our behalf, and without these prayers we don't know where we, or our boys, would be.

It is a joy to conclude this work as I return home with my little boys, since they are for me the greatest testimony and reminder of God's blessing and ability to accomplish the impossible. A little more than a year after hearing something was "impossible" – namely having children – God sent two boys, each born within the current abortion bracket, a testimony to life over death.

Epilogue

My heart froze.

"Take off your belt, your shoes, your watch, and any other metallic items," said the prison officer abruptly, as I returned to HMP Glenochil.

I couldn't believe it: I was back. How did this happen? I had a wife back home with two beautiful boys. Almost a decade had passed since I'd last passed through these gates in 2006. Since then I'd obtained a theology degree as well as a diploma, and spent years trying to help others avoid places like this. But I was back in the very prison where Matt had nearly been killed, the prison where I had almost killed another in revenge.

Now I was returning, not as a convict, but as a Prison Mentor, tasked with helping other men leave a life of crime behind.

"Okay, come on through, sir," said another officer. Barely a few hundred yards from where I was now standing, I had cried out to God from within the solitary walls of this prison. Now I was sat in the waiting room with lawyers and other professionals, social workers and agents. All I could do was marvel at the mercy of God as I waited to see another man whom society had written off.

I just smiled, remembering that, "With God all things are possible" (Matthew 19:26).

Notes

1. "HM INSPECTORATE OF PRISONS: Report on HM Young Offenders Institution Polmont", August 2004, paras 2.10–2.12. Available at http://www.gov.scot/Publicatio ns/2004/08/19688/40570 (accessed 2 April 2016).

2. "HM INSPECTORATE OF PRISONS: Report on HM Young Offenders Institution Polmont", para 2.28.

3. Dietrich Bonhoeffer, *Life Together: The Classic Exploration of Christian Community*, New York: Harper & Row, 1954.

4. Catechism of the Catholic Church, paragraph 1324. Available at http://www.bbc.co.uk/news/uk-northern-ireland-36278250

Glossary

Bam – idiot.

Camp – the gang or group of convicts you associate with. In the Young Offenders' institutions, camps are usually determined by geographical locations, e.g. Glasgow lads or Edinburgh lads. Within the adult jails, these groups are usually determined by choice, and are important indicators of a convict's status within the prison's social structure.

Co-pilot – cellmate.

Digger – solitary confinement: to be diggered is to be sent to solitary confinement.

Dog squad – in the context of prison, a particularly brutal group of officers.

NIC – National Induction Centre.

Scheme – a housing estate.

Screws – prison officers.

Slip the jab – to dodge a punch.

Spy hatch – steel shutter on the outside of the cell door that allowed prison officers to look into the cell.

Square go – a one-on-one fight, as opposed to both sides fighting.

Tool – a weapon.

Weegies – Glaswegians.

YOs – young offenders.

Out of the Ashes

*"One of the most compelling biographies
I have ever read."*
- **Carl Beech,** The Message Trust

Peter Gladwin was barely one
when a domestic fire left him partly
disabled and horribly scarred.
The third of nine children, he was
raised on a rough council estate
in Halifax. Peter was always in
trouble. Then he was stabbed and
effectively lost the use of his right
arm. Every relationship failed.
For years Peter took refuge in
gambling, drinking and drugs.

After Peter contemplated suicide, a conversation with his
elder sister led to an encounter that would change his life
forever...

It was the start of a profound transformation.

ISBN 978-1-85424-992-0 | e-ISBN 978-0-85721-240-5

www.lionhudson.com

Jail Bird

"Totally gripping"
- Chris Evans,
BBC Radio 2, Presenter

What led a glamourous radio presenter, Sharon Grenham-Thompson, to get involved with working with some of the most despised in society – prisoners?

As an Anglican priest, Sharon could have stayed well outside the prison walls – but in fact she felt herself drawn to working in Bedford jail.

Recognising that those who commit crimes, even the most horrible ones, are still human, she drew on years of feeling that she didn't fit in either.

It may be a far cry from appearing on BBC Radio 2, but she managed to integrate her two very different worlds, and in this fascinating book, she invites her readers to join her.

ISBN 978-0-7459-6877-3 | e-ISBN 978-0-7459-6878-0

www.lionhudson.com